PATTERNS

by

PATTY

A Coloring Book

ISBN: 978-1-951576-12-7

~Cover Art Created by~
Patricia Burke

~Cover Art Colored by Colorist~
Jean Riendeau

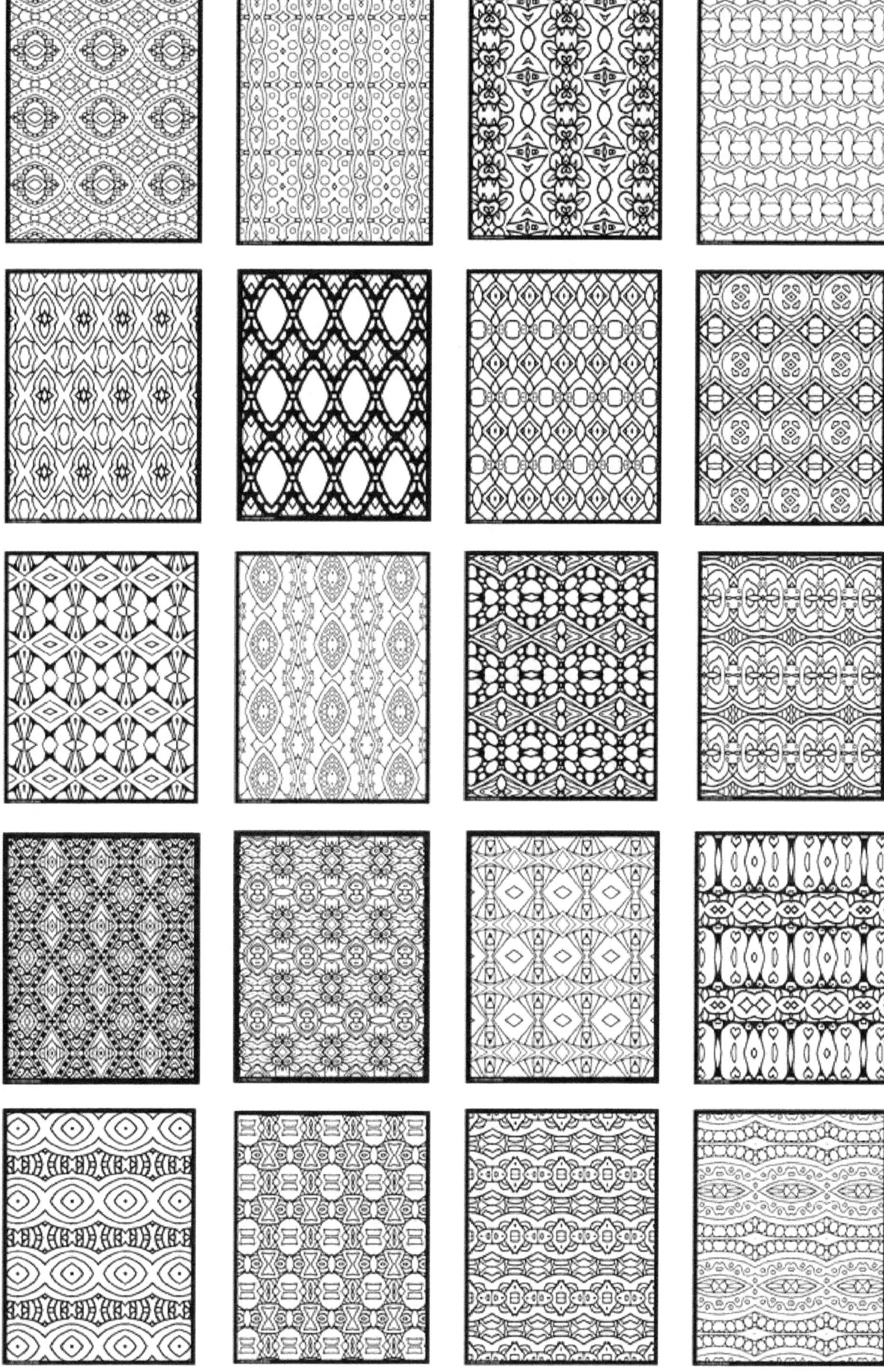

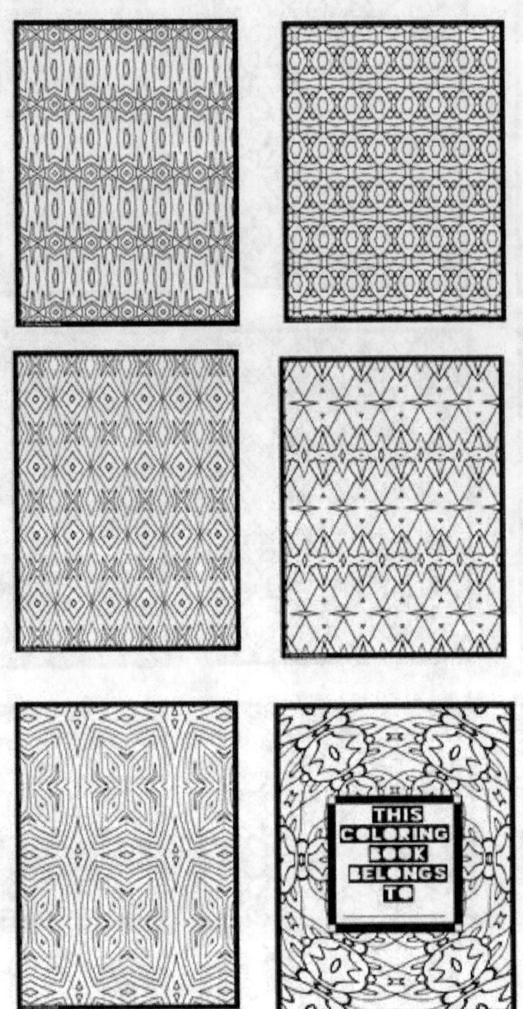
THIS
COLORING
BOOK
BELONGS
TO

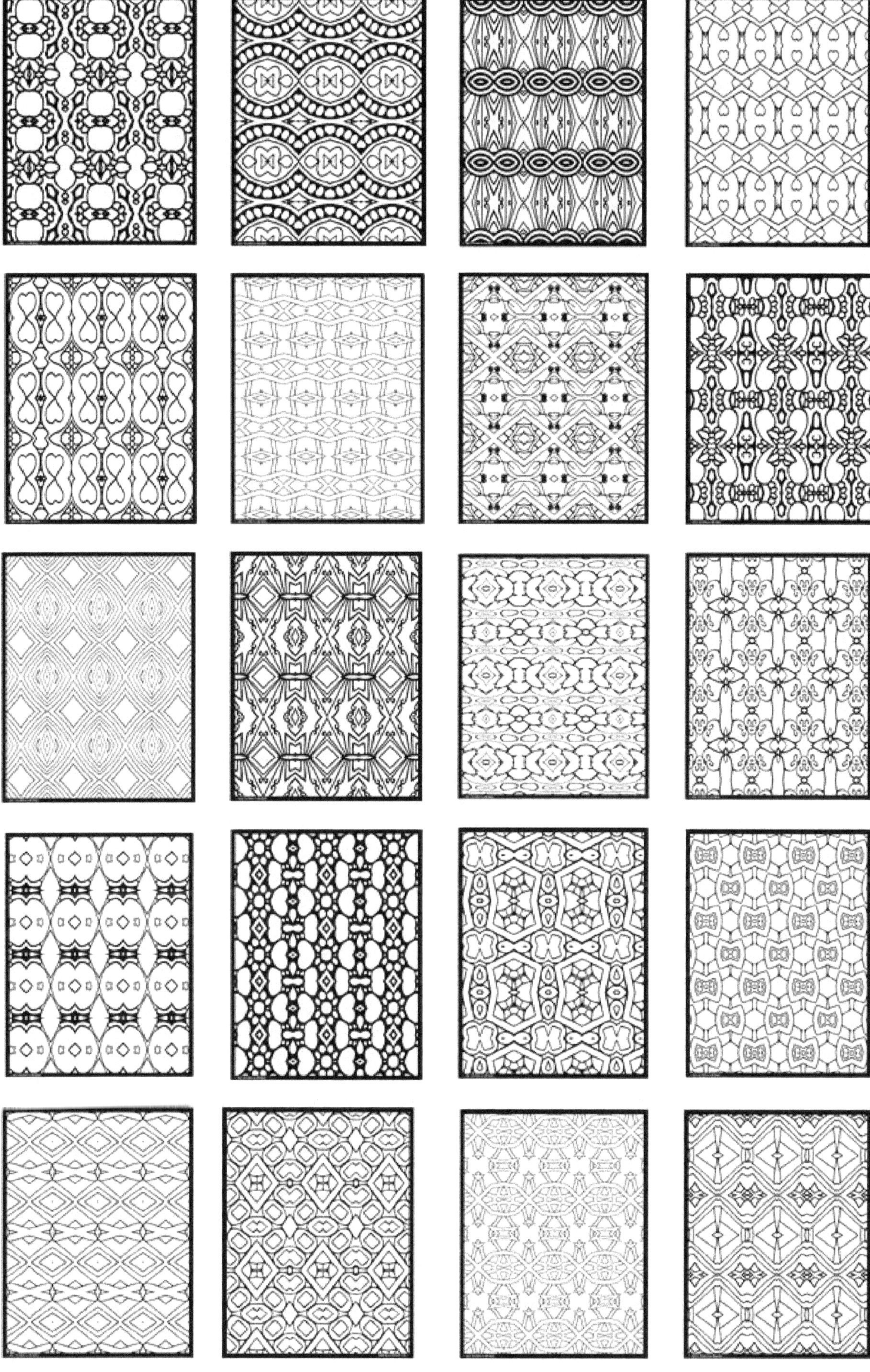

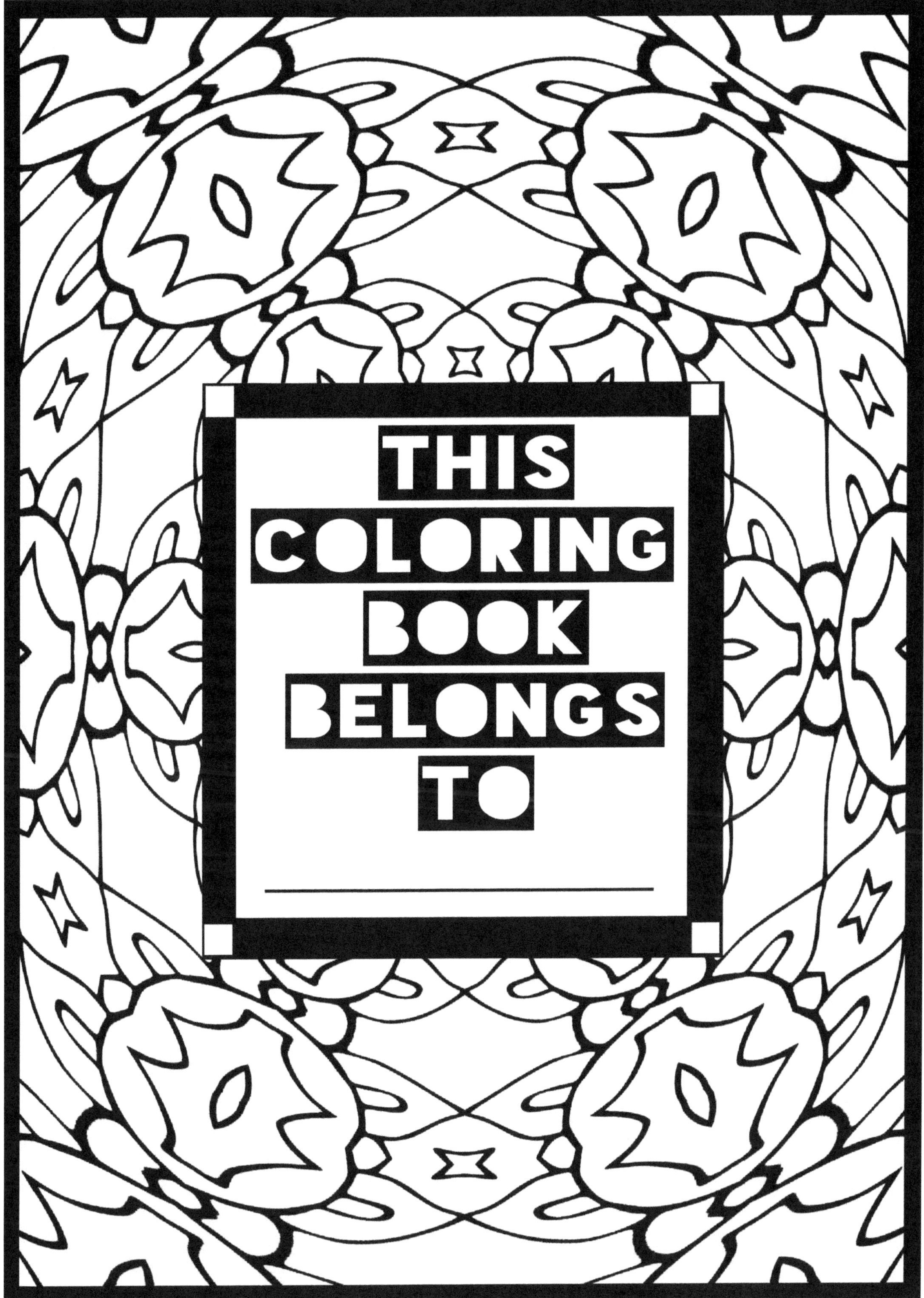
THIS
COLORING
BOOK
BELONGS
TO

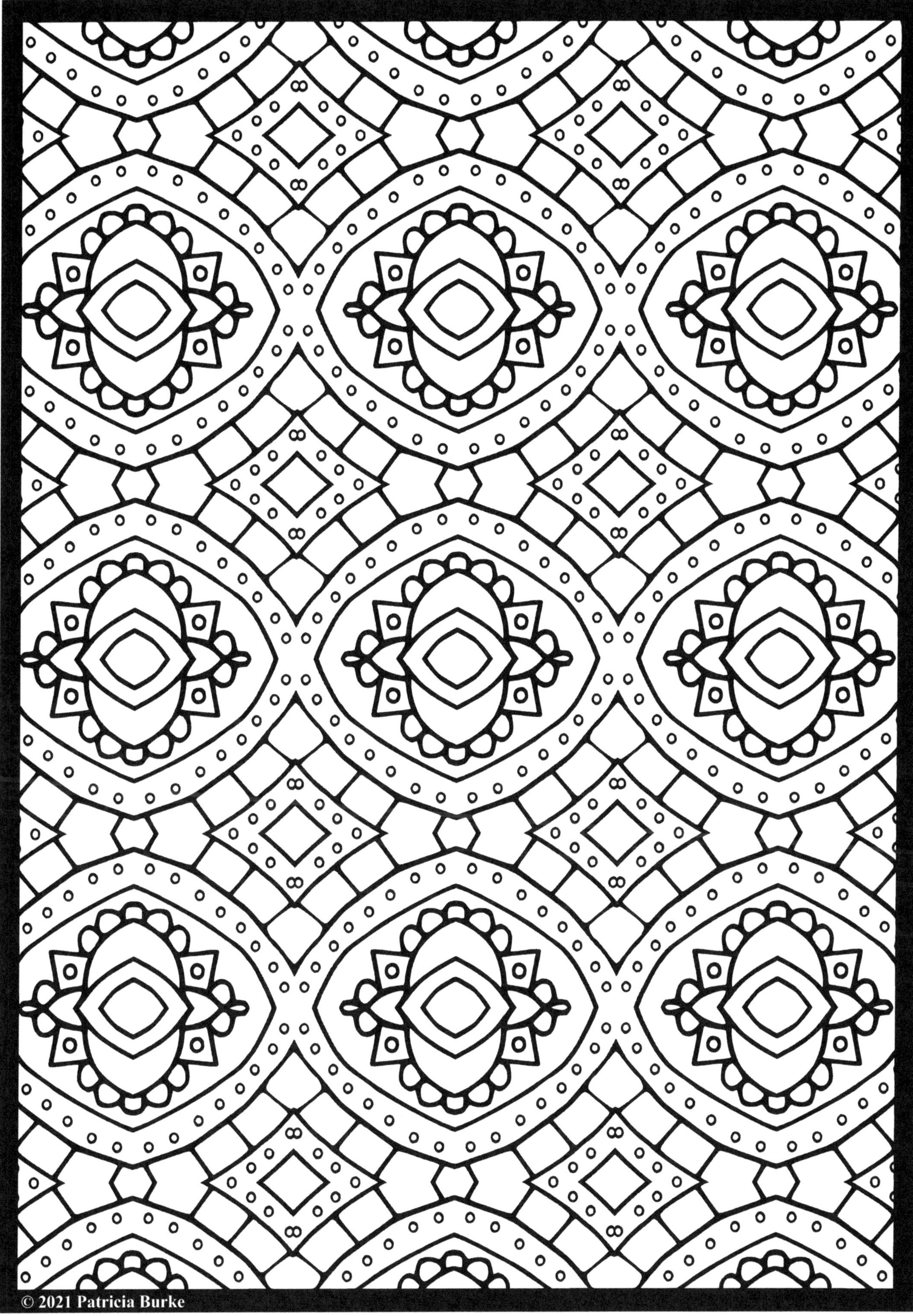

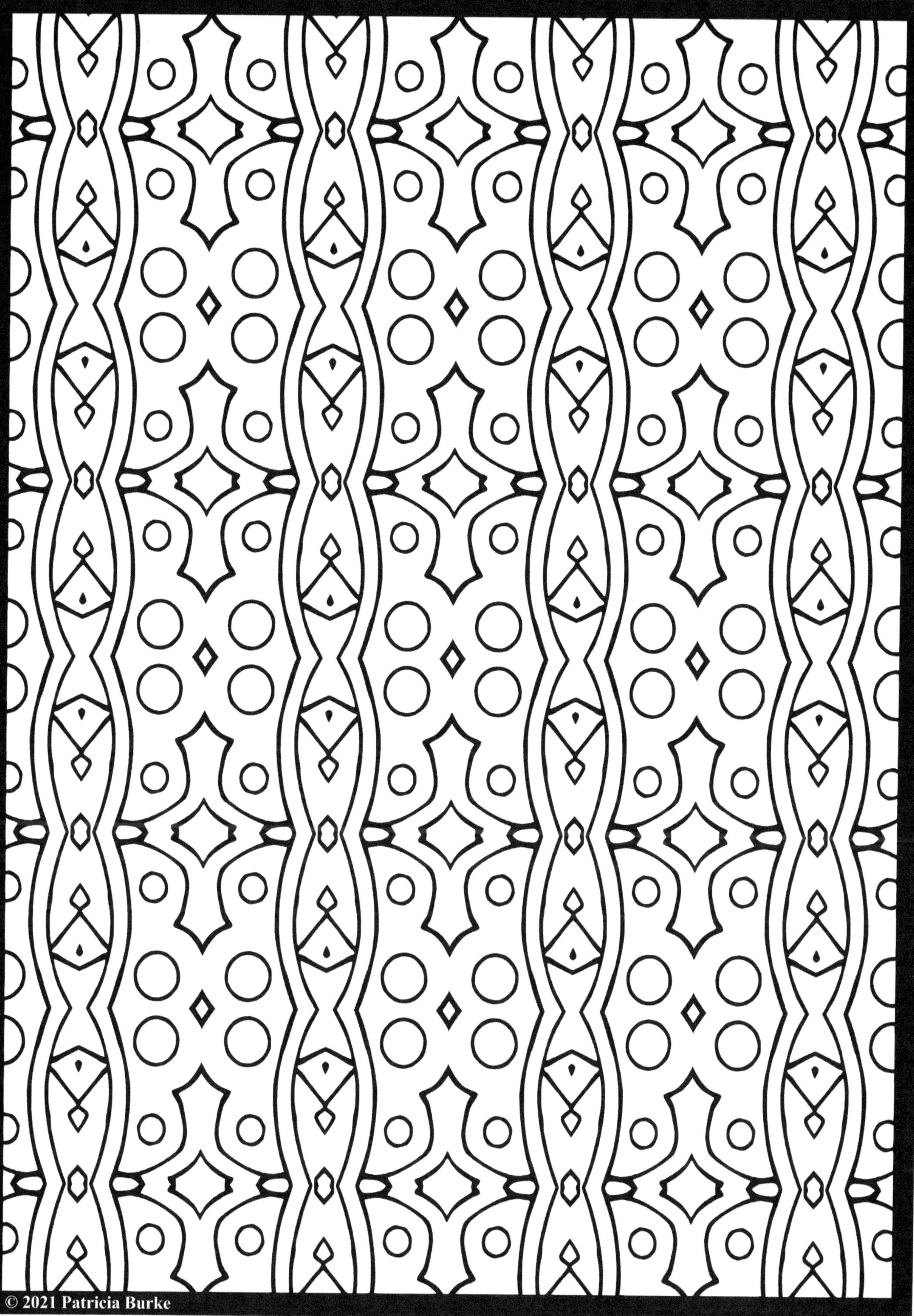

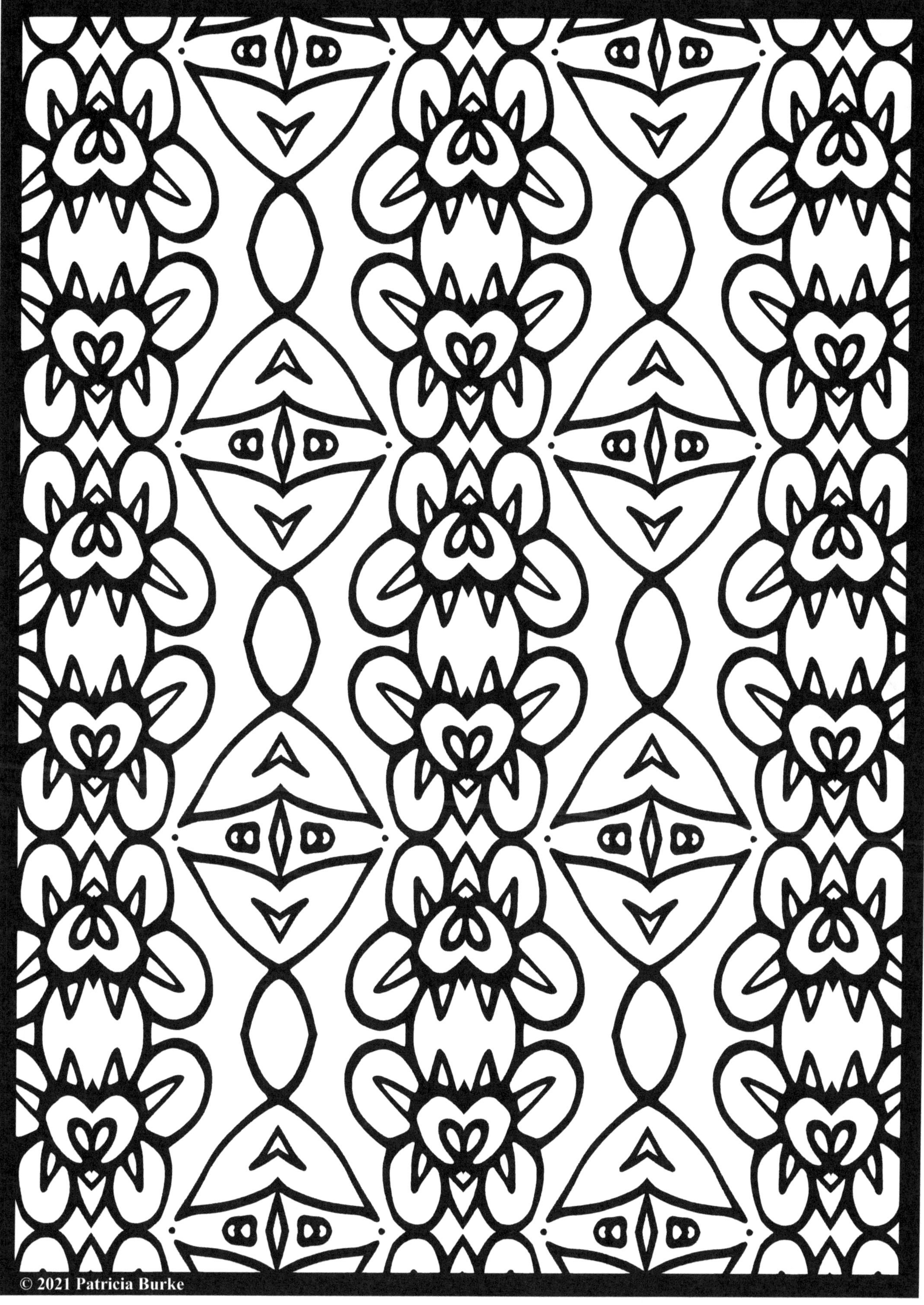

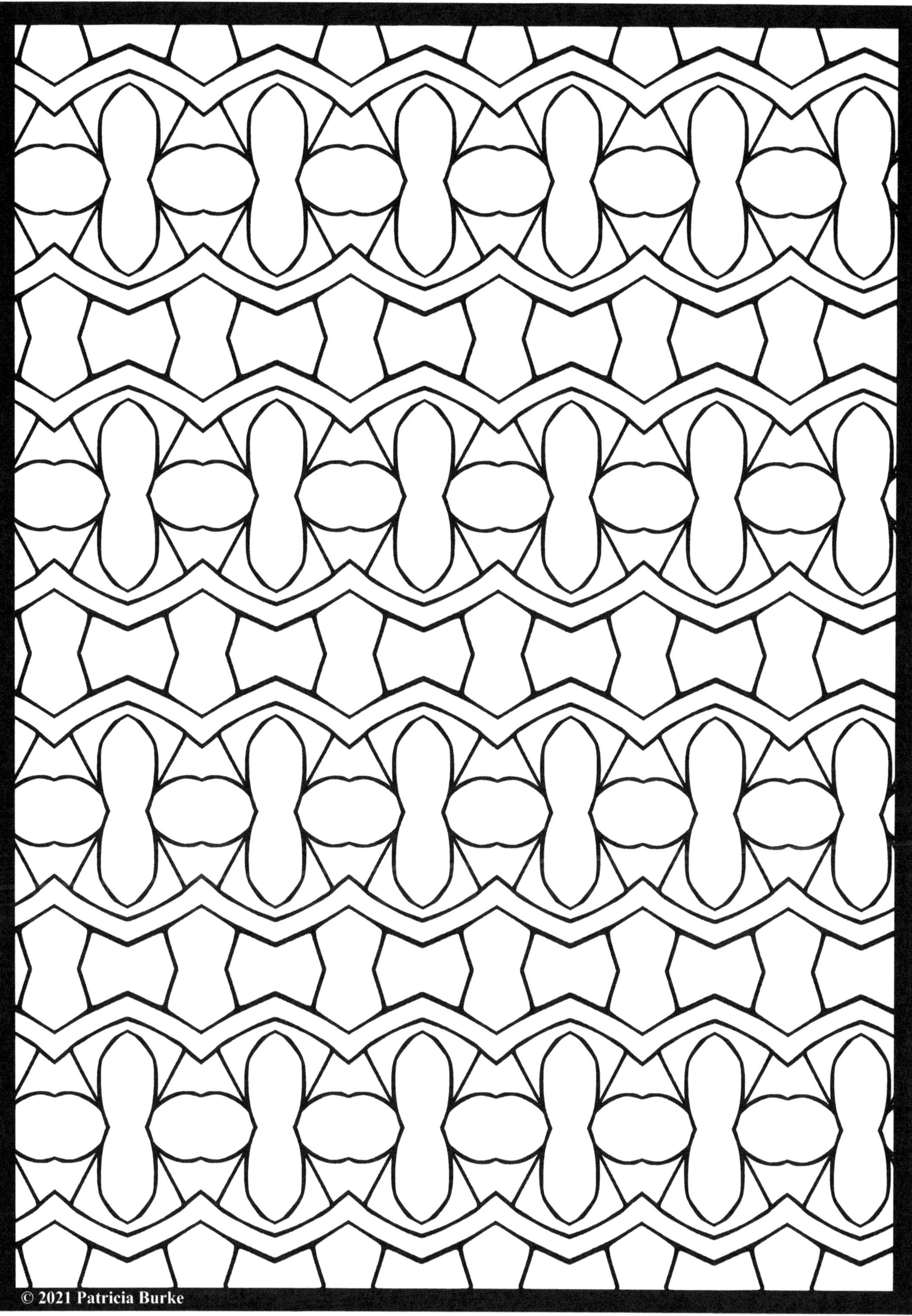

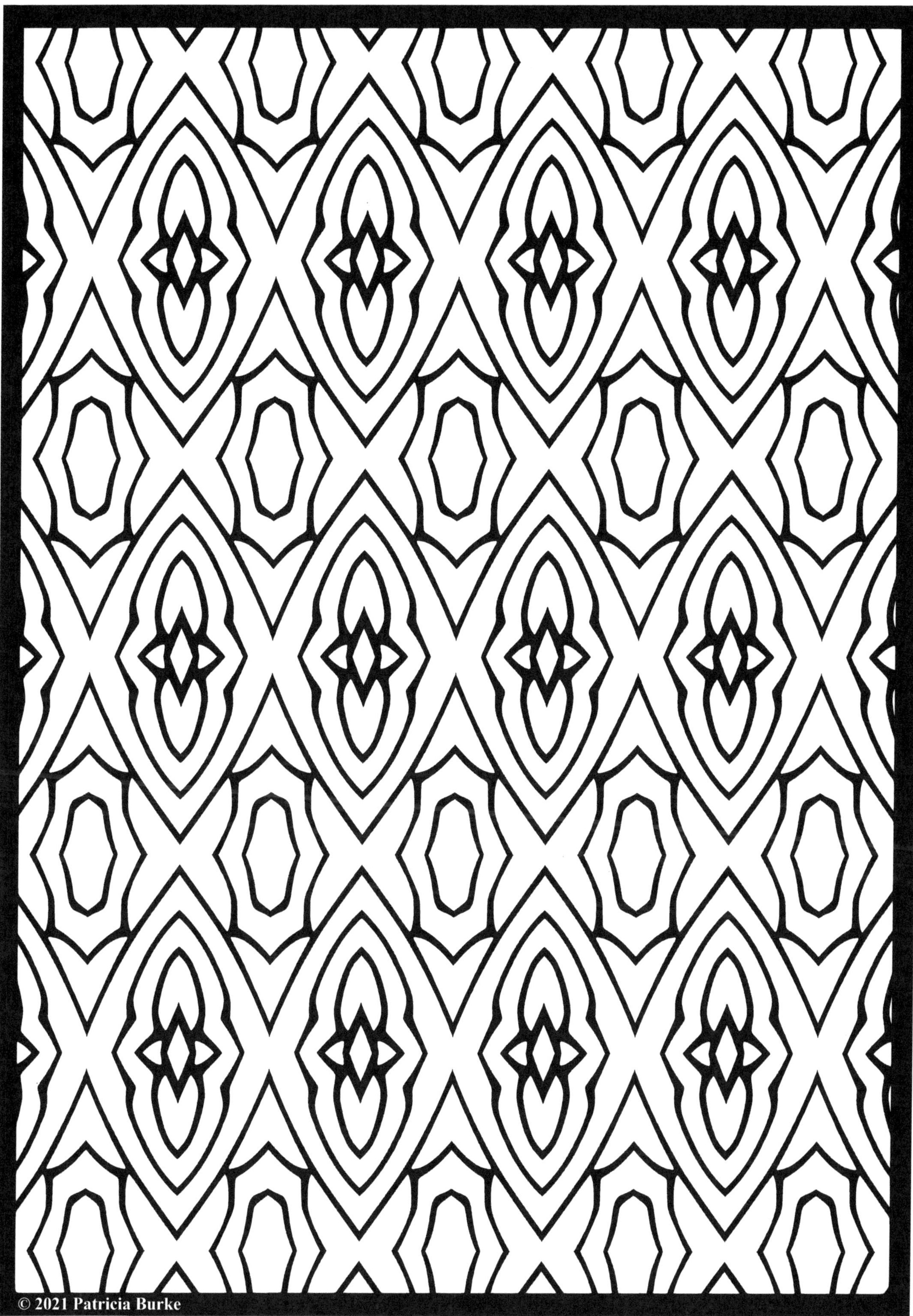

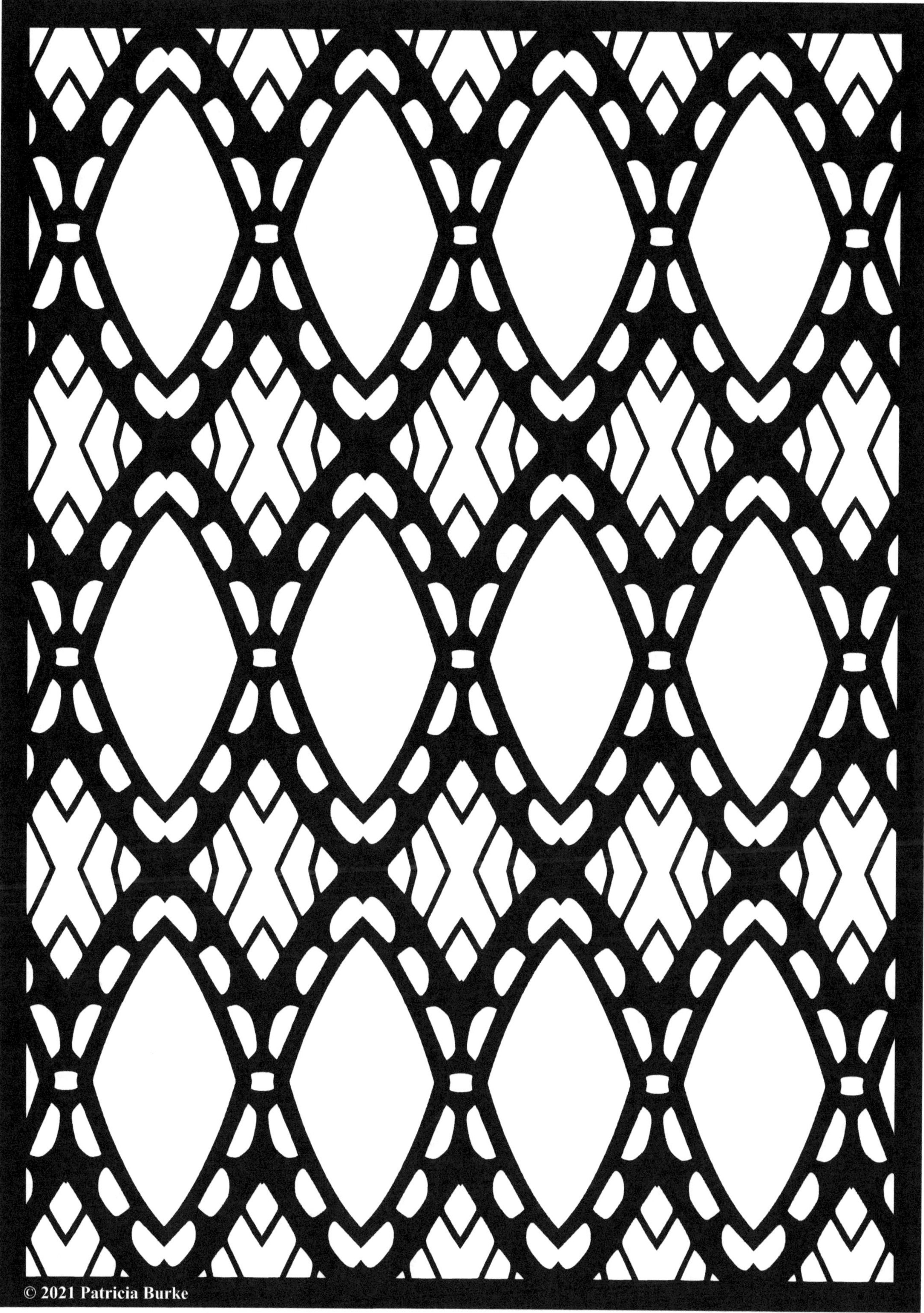

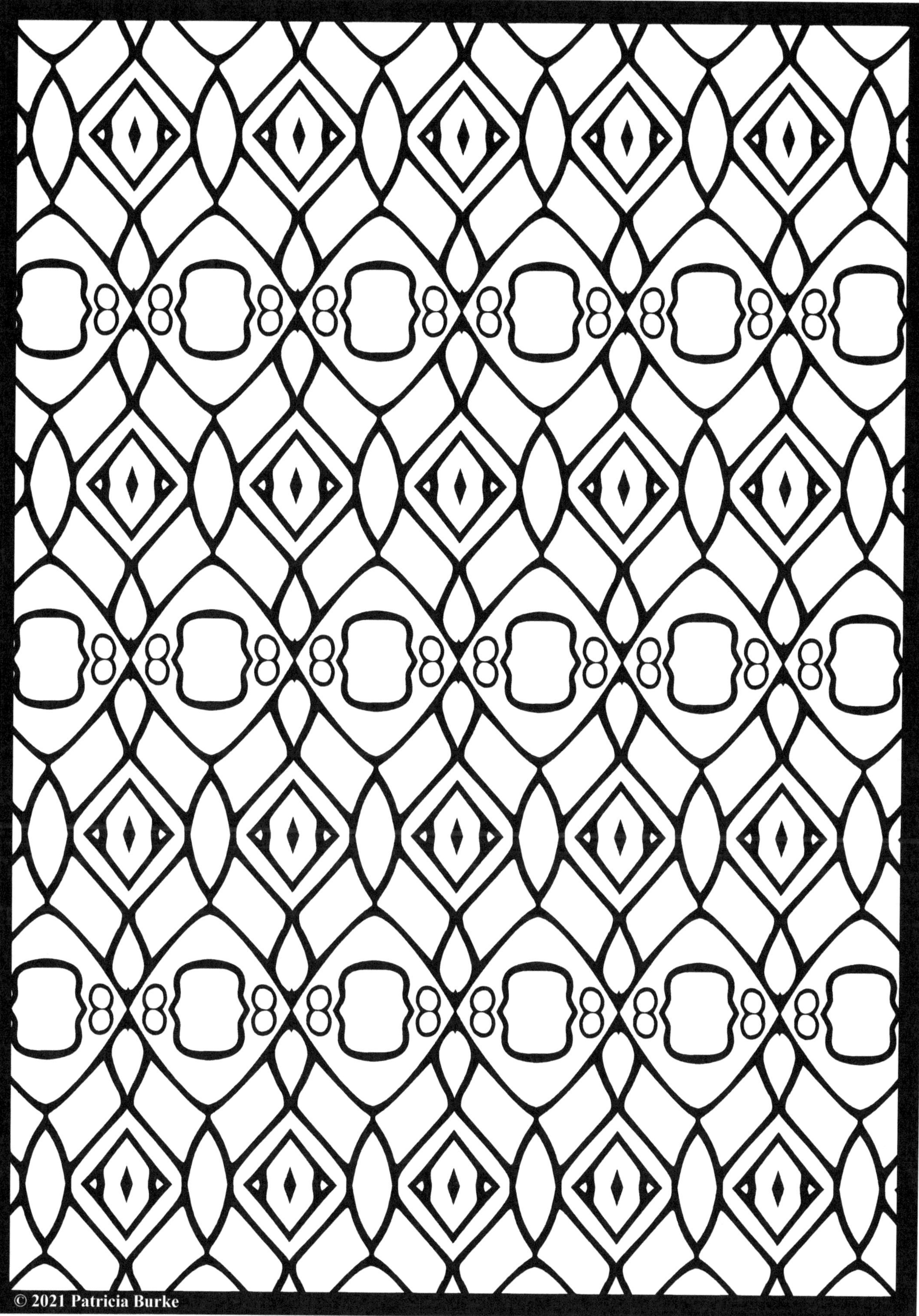

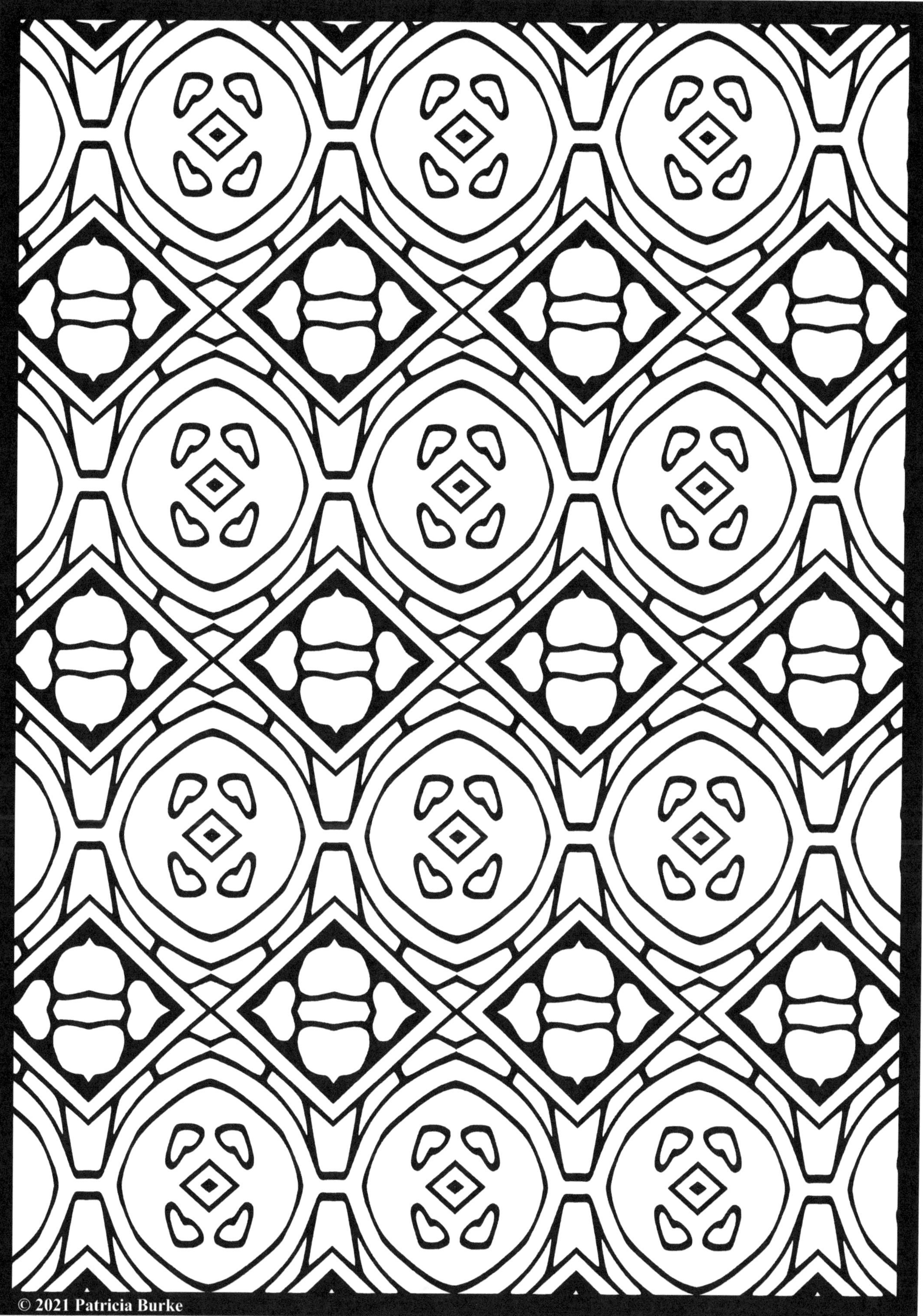

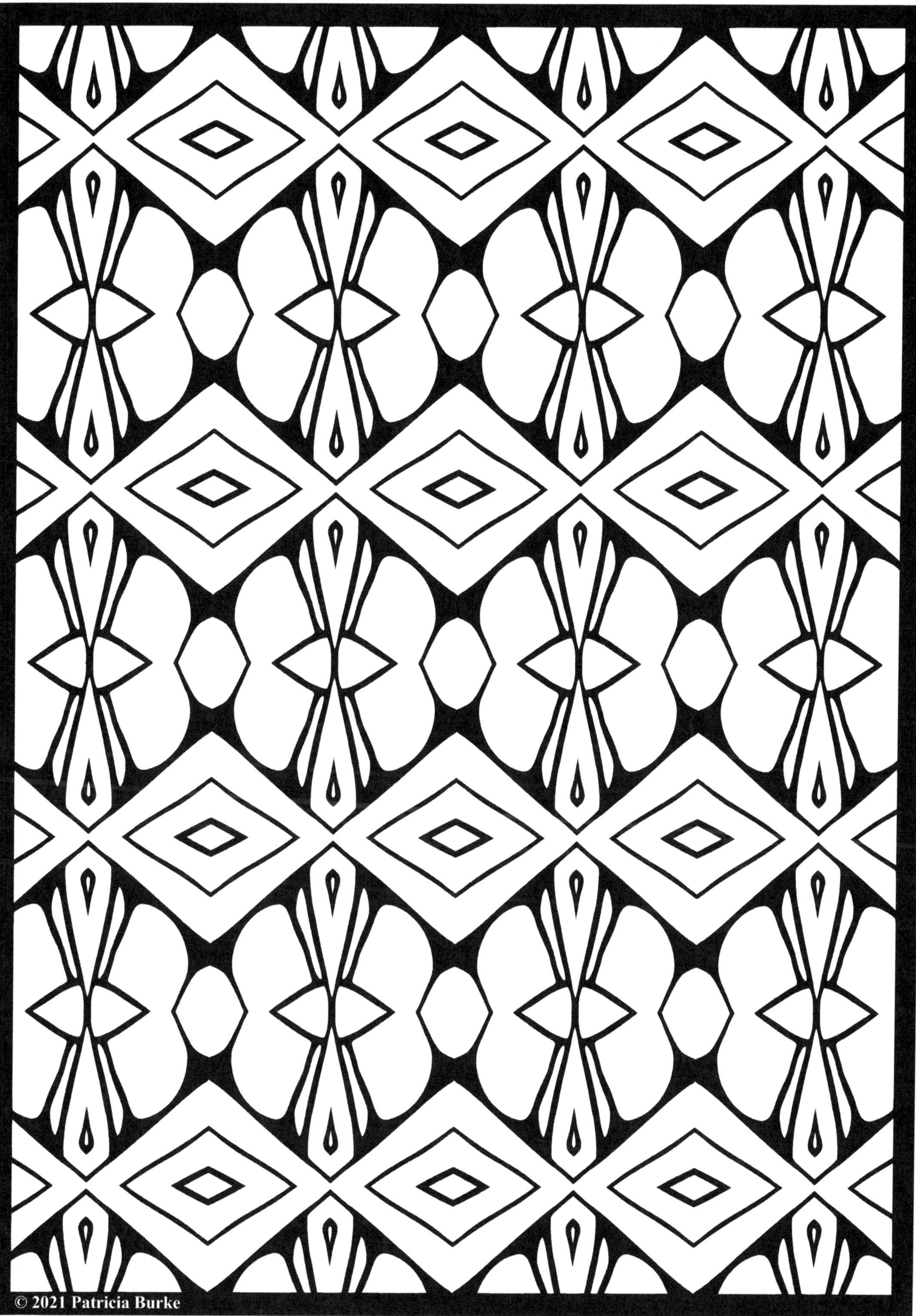

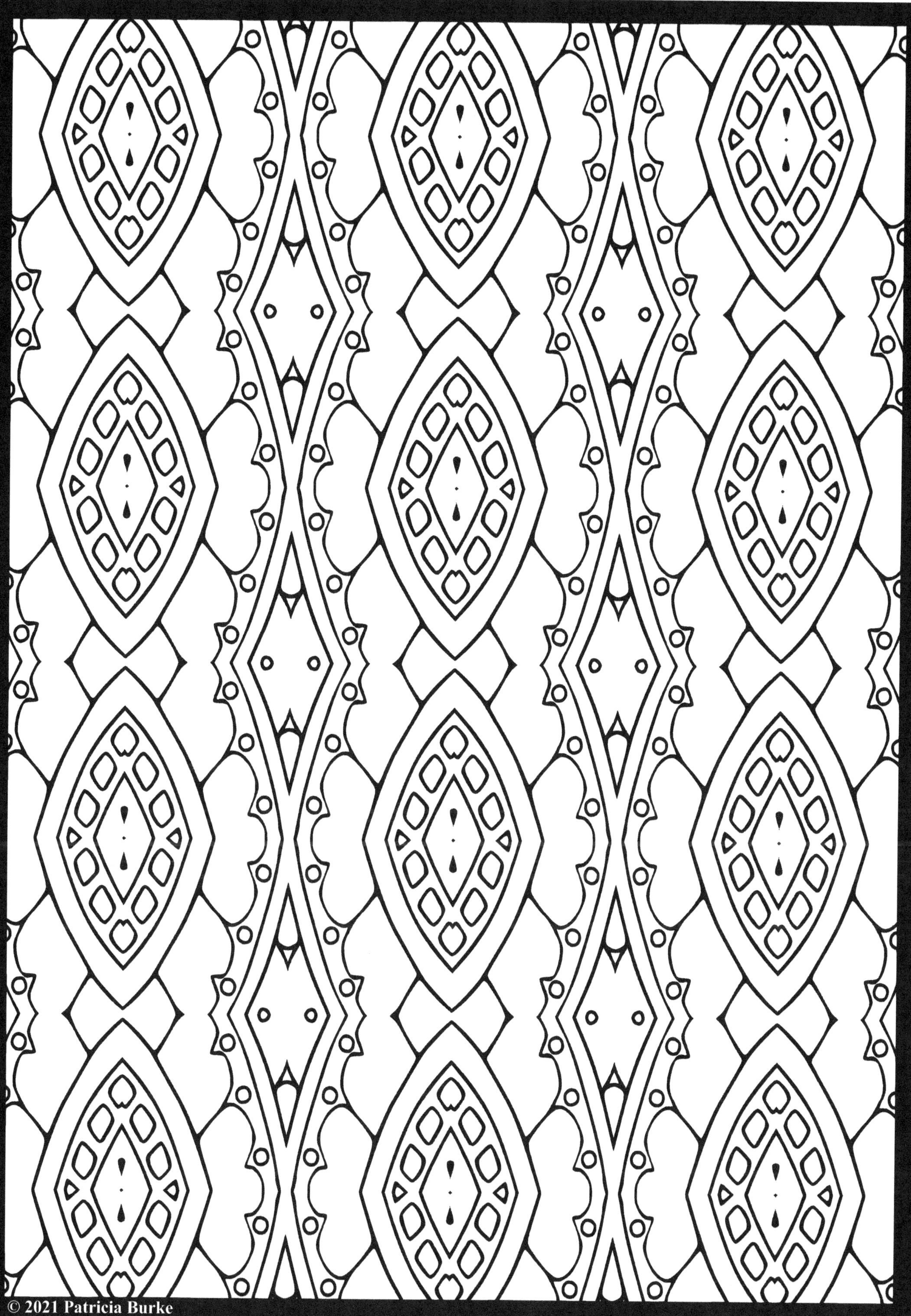

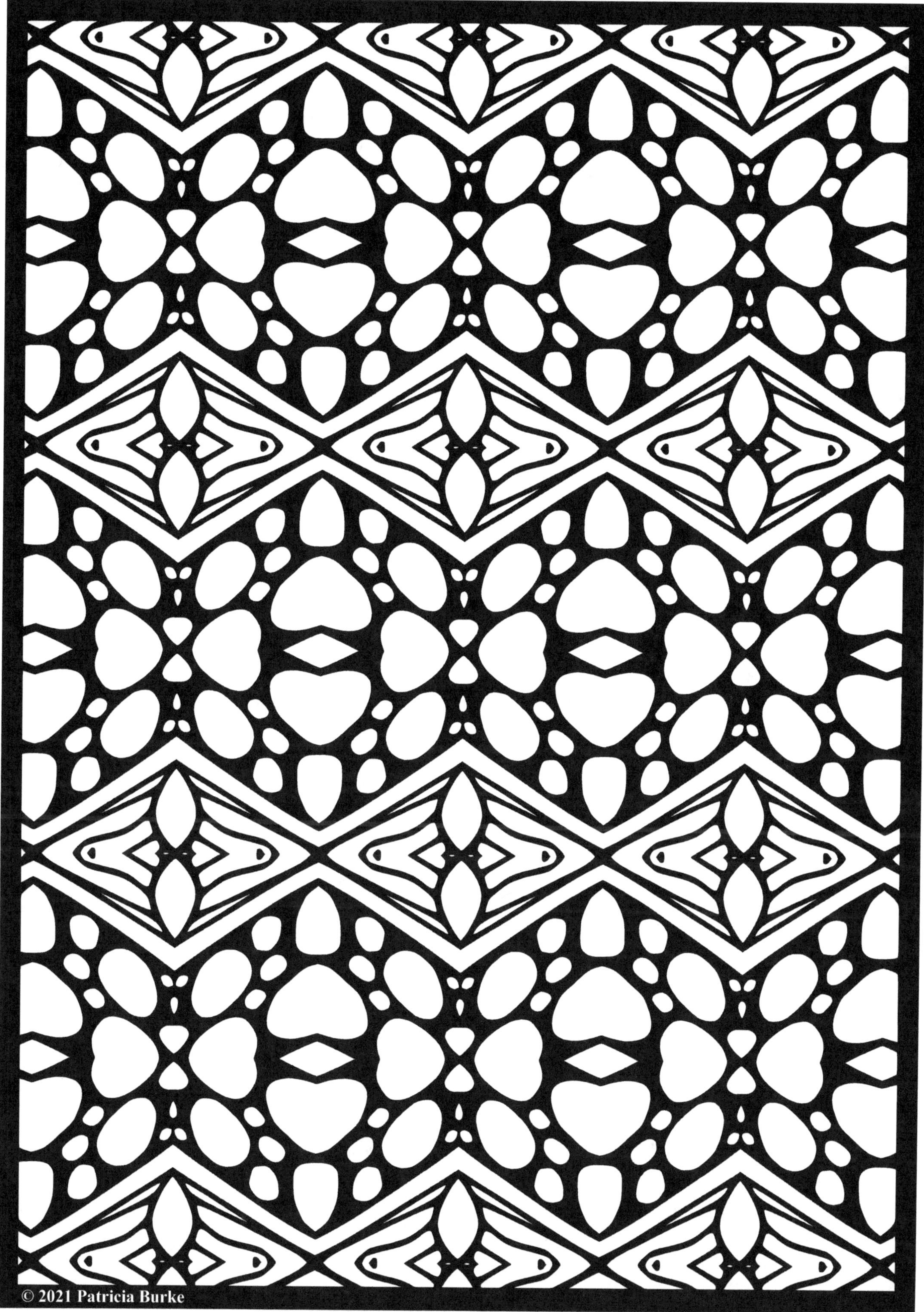

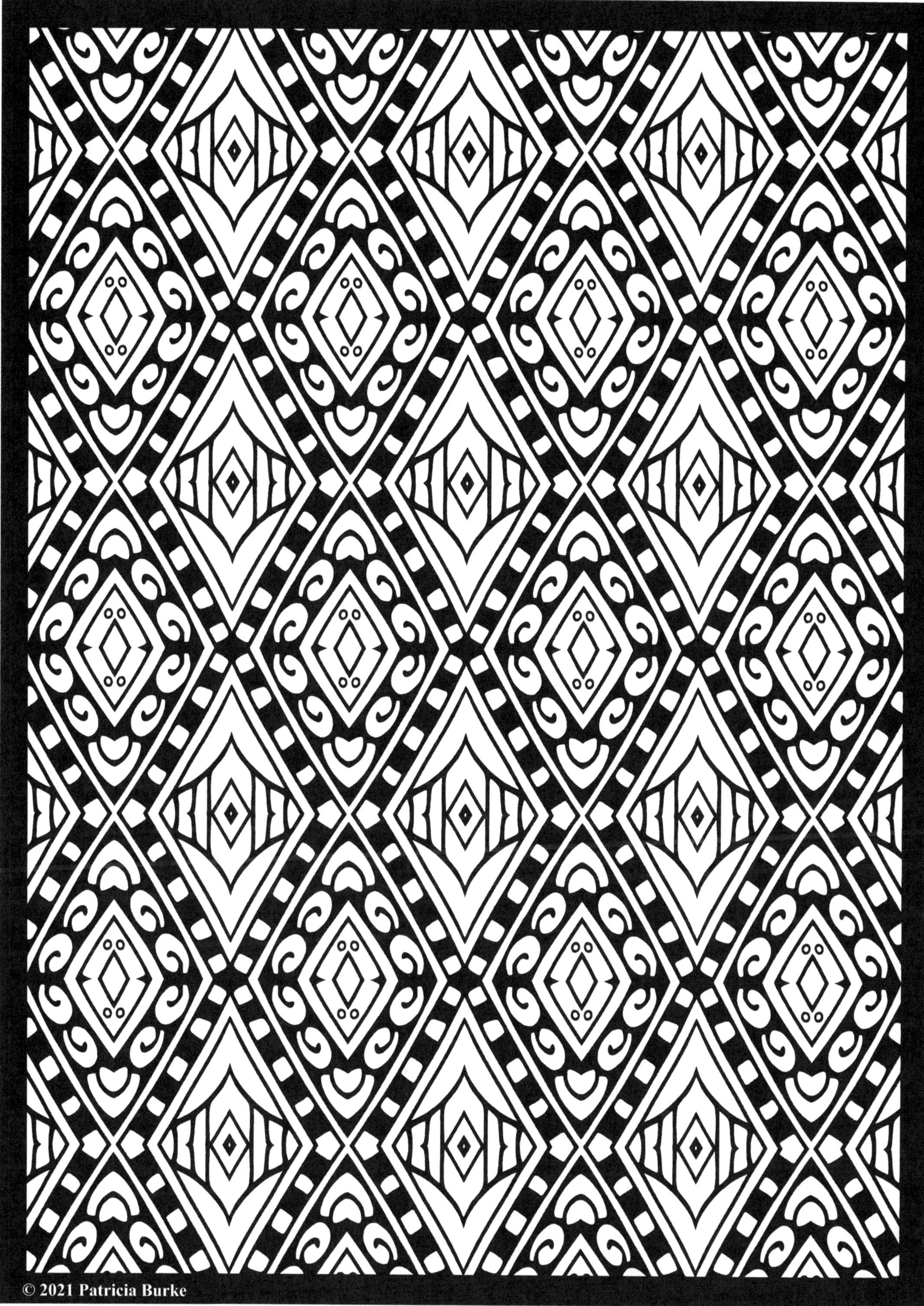

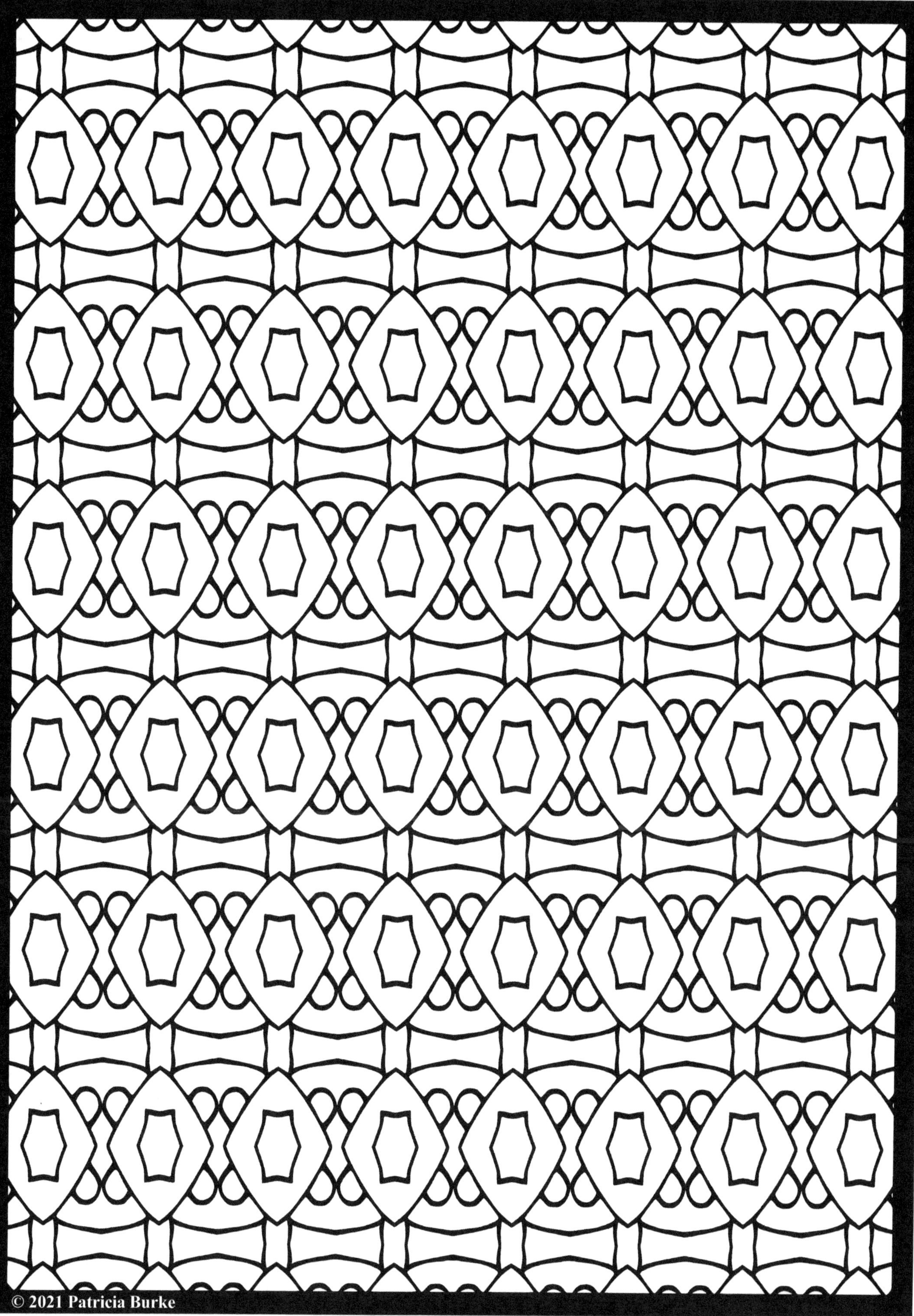

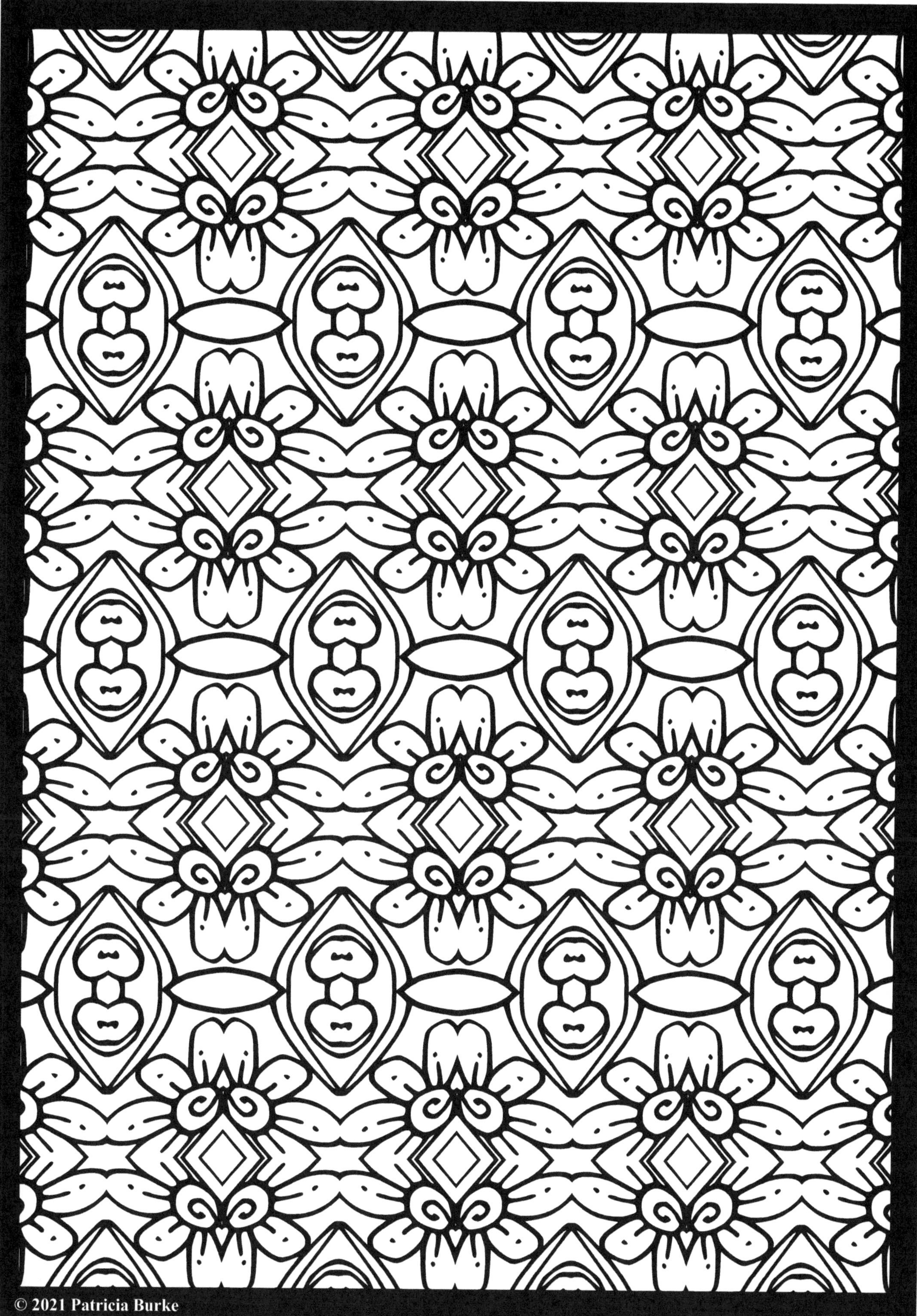

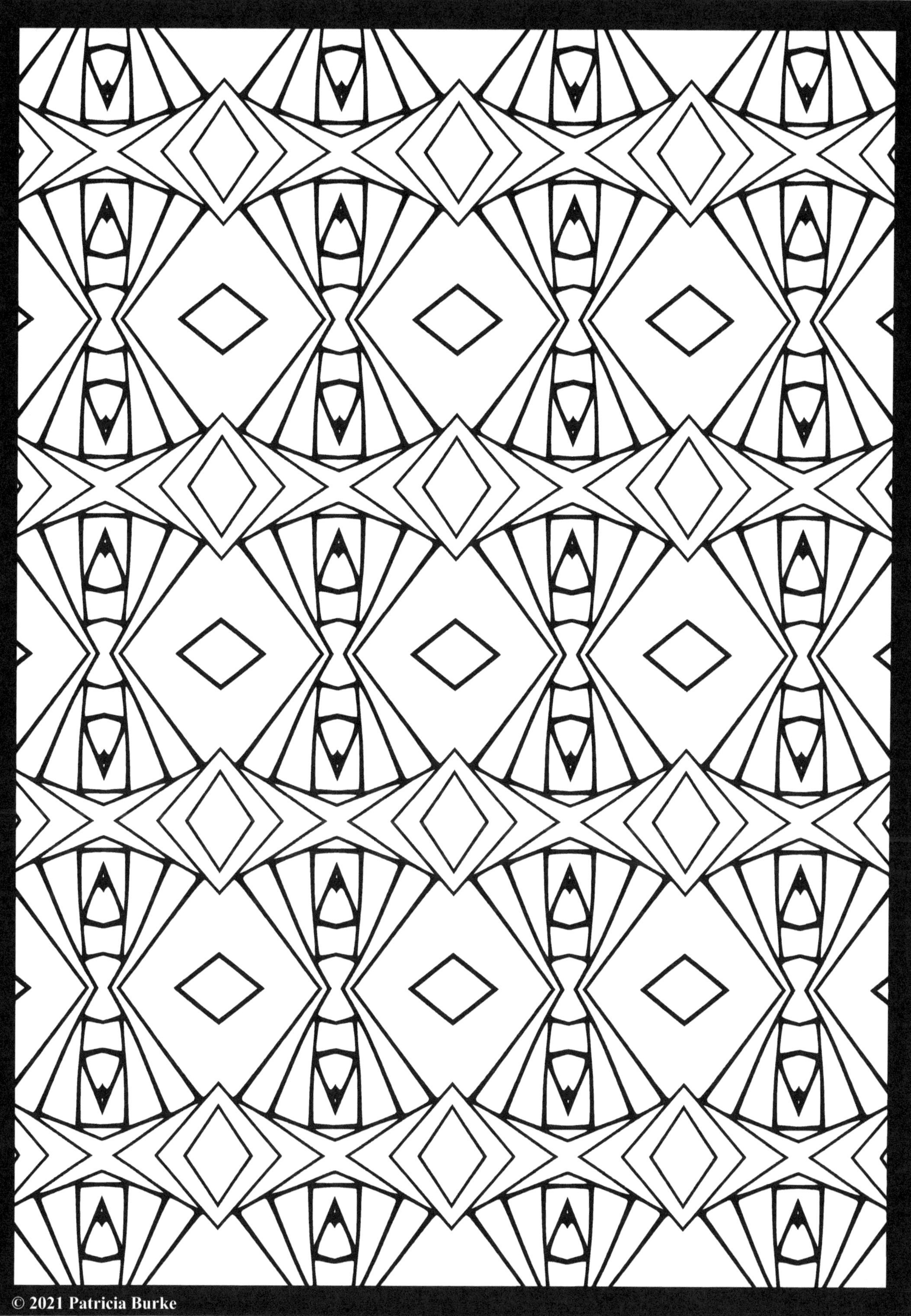

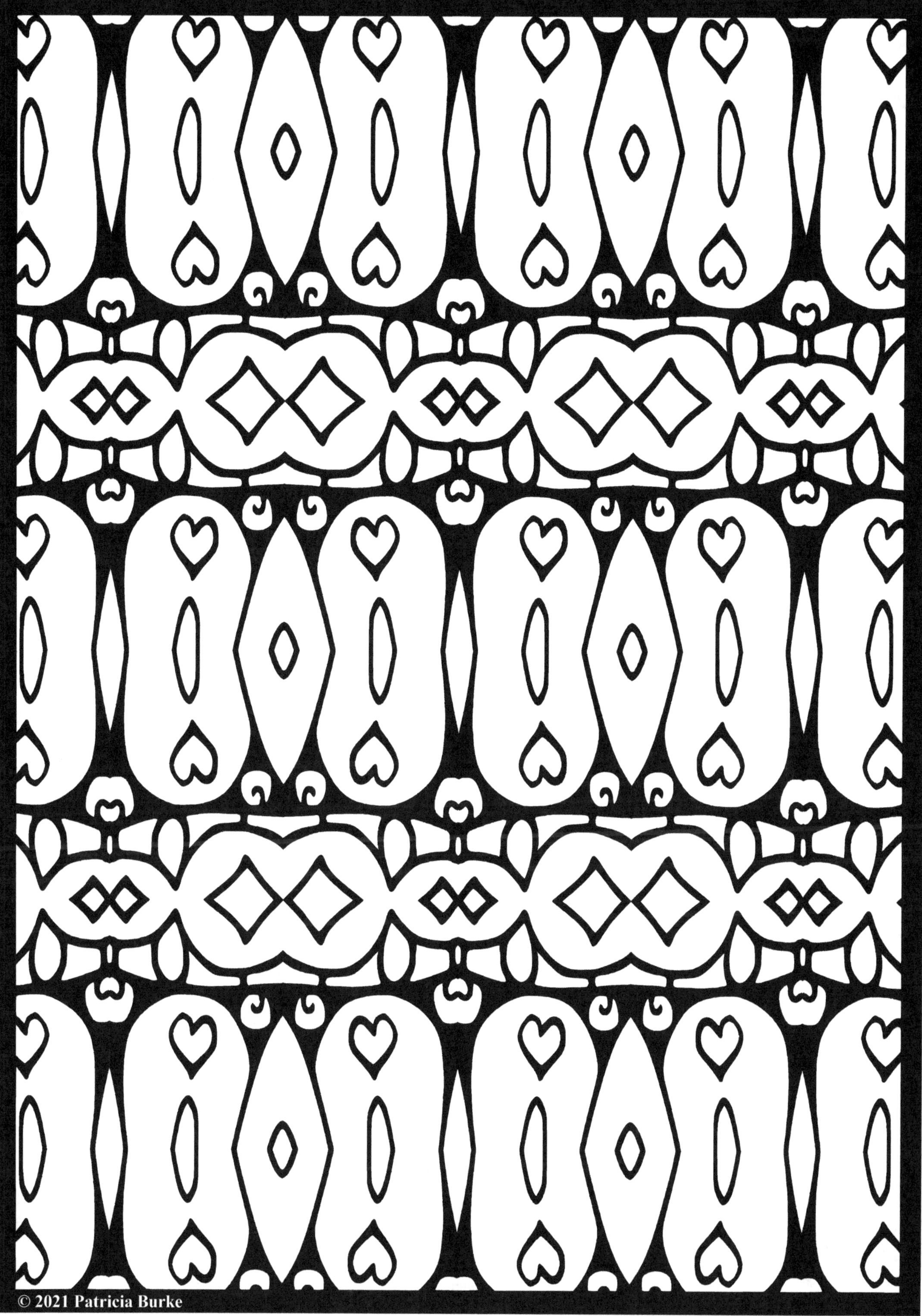

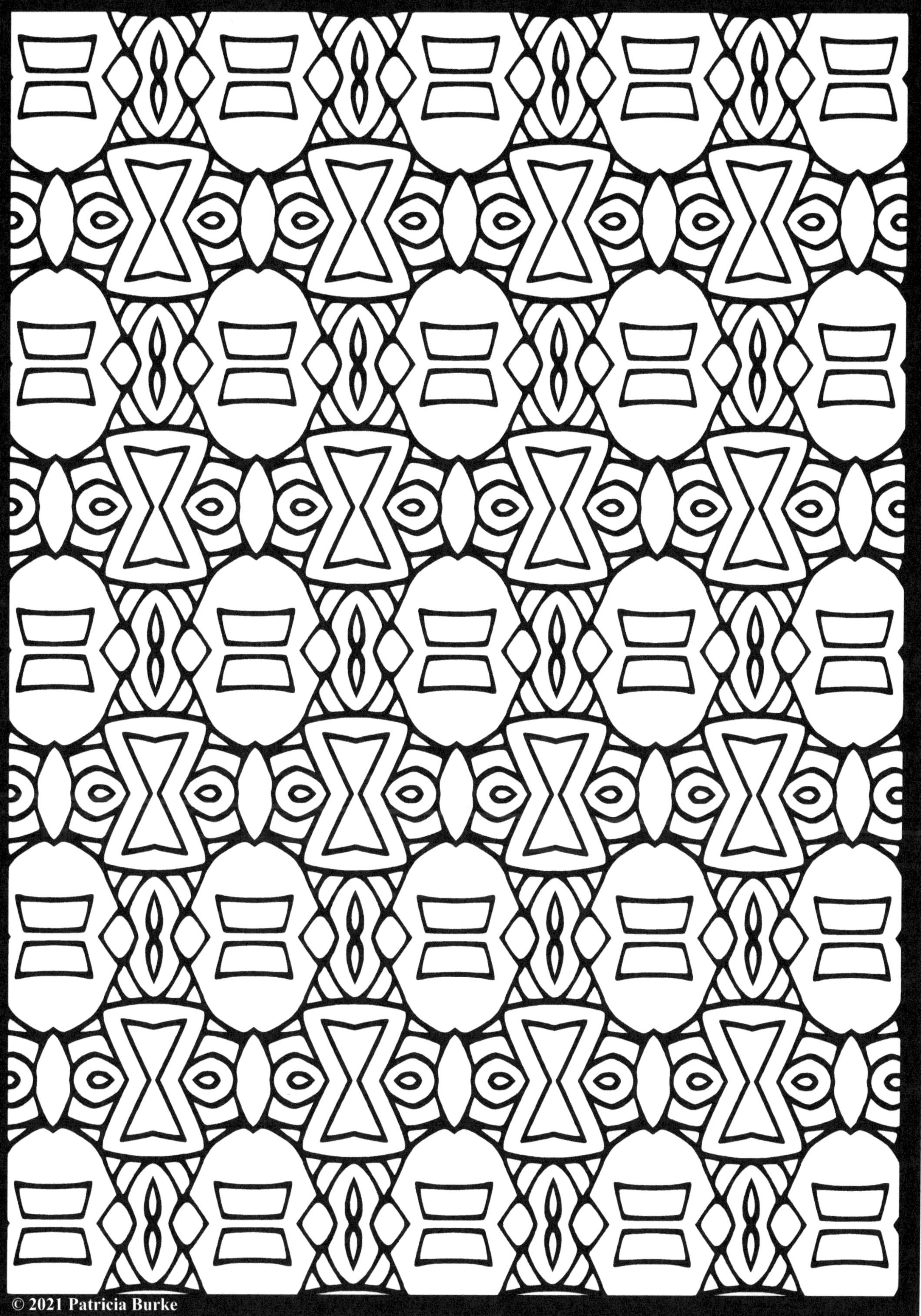

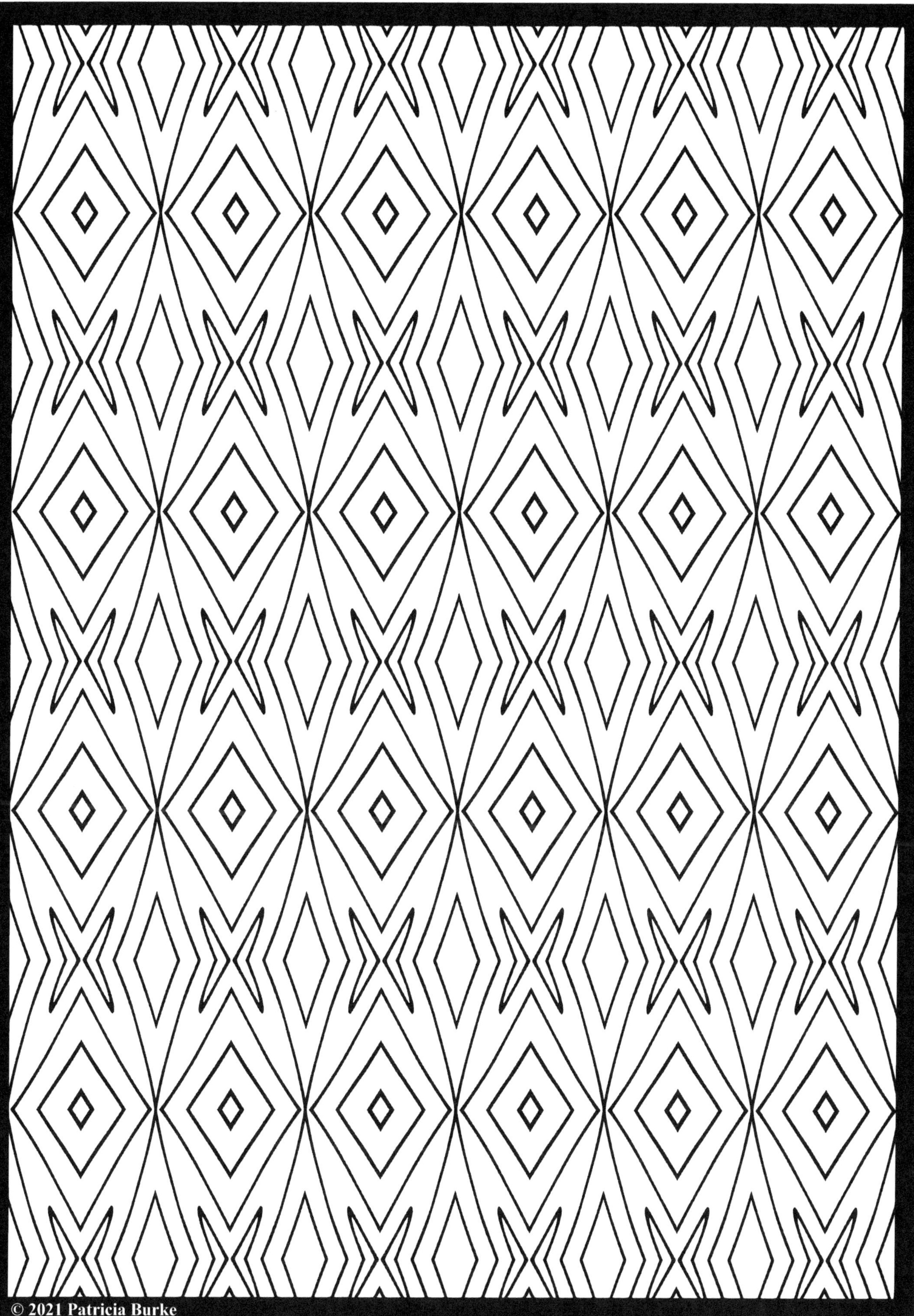

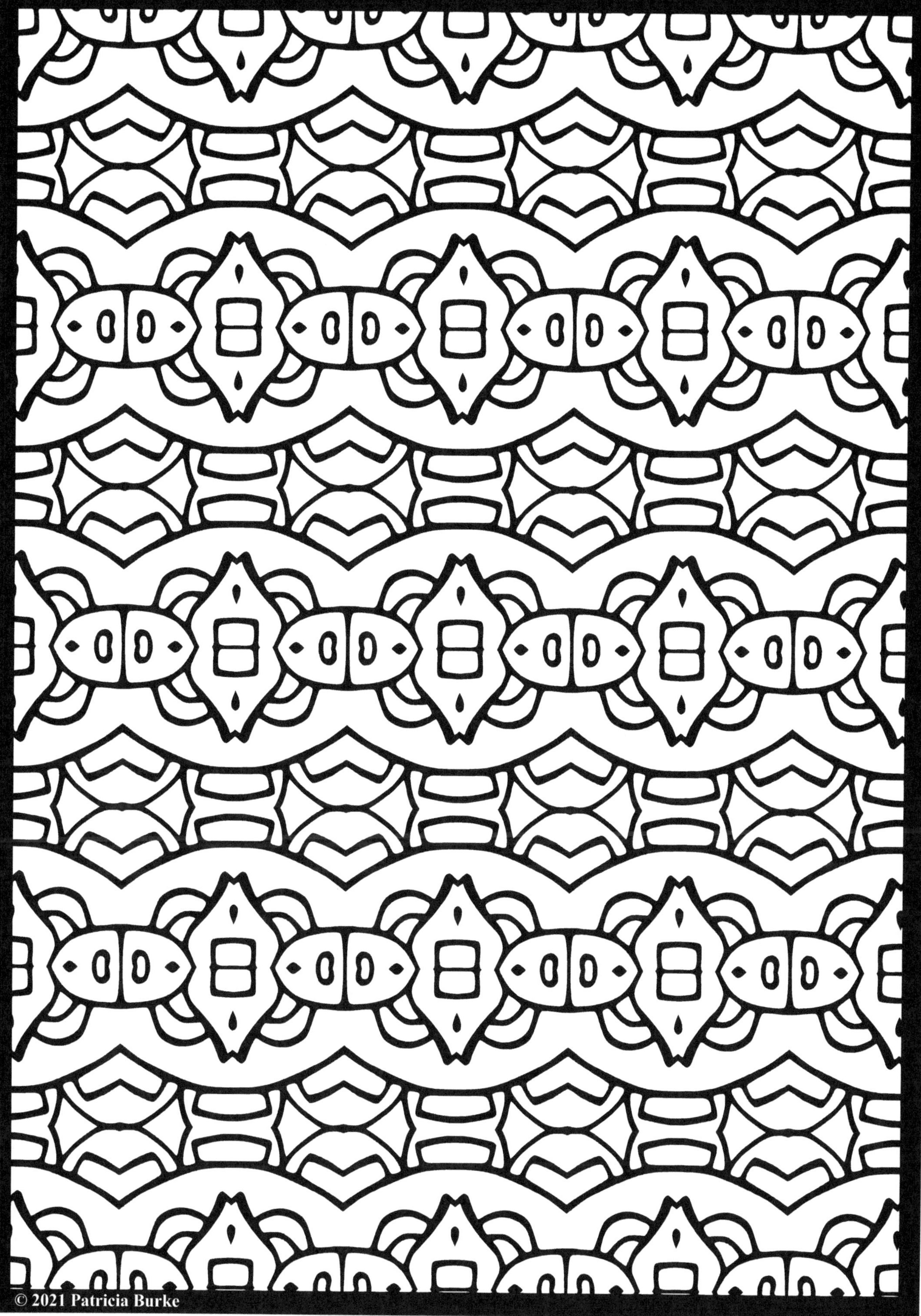

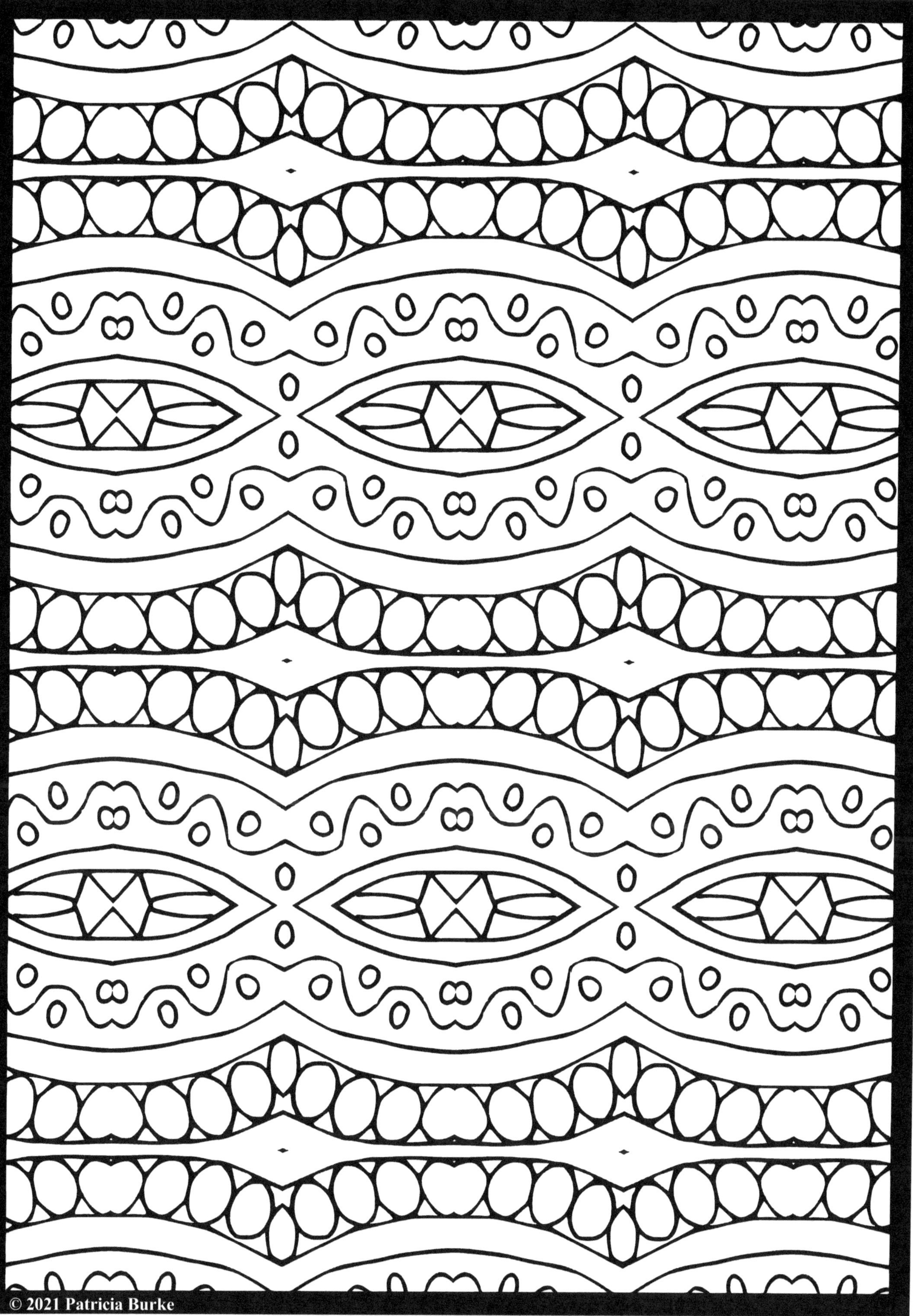

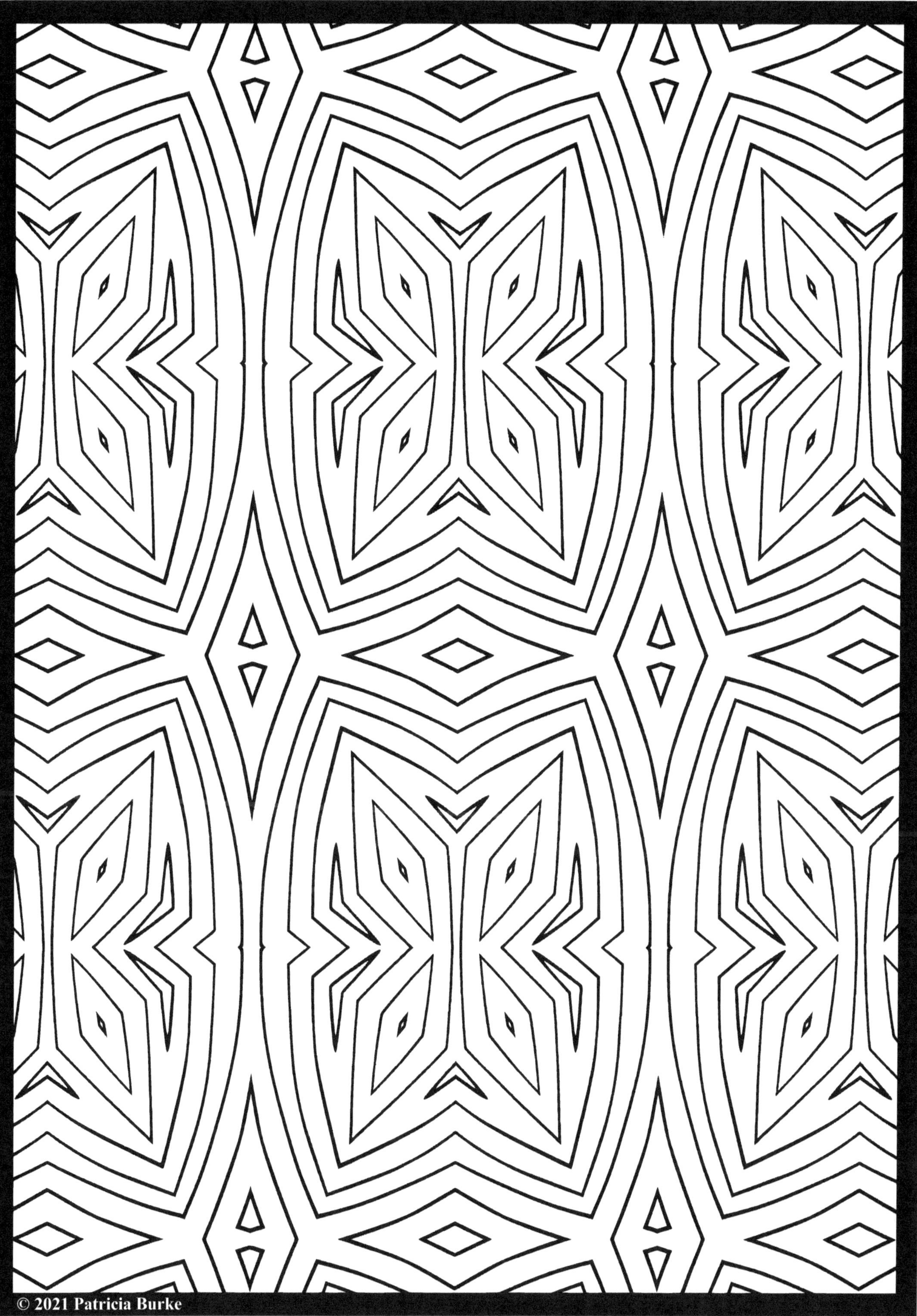

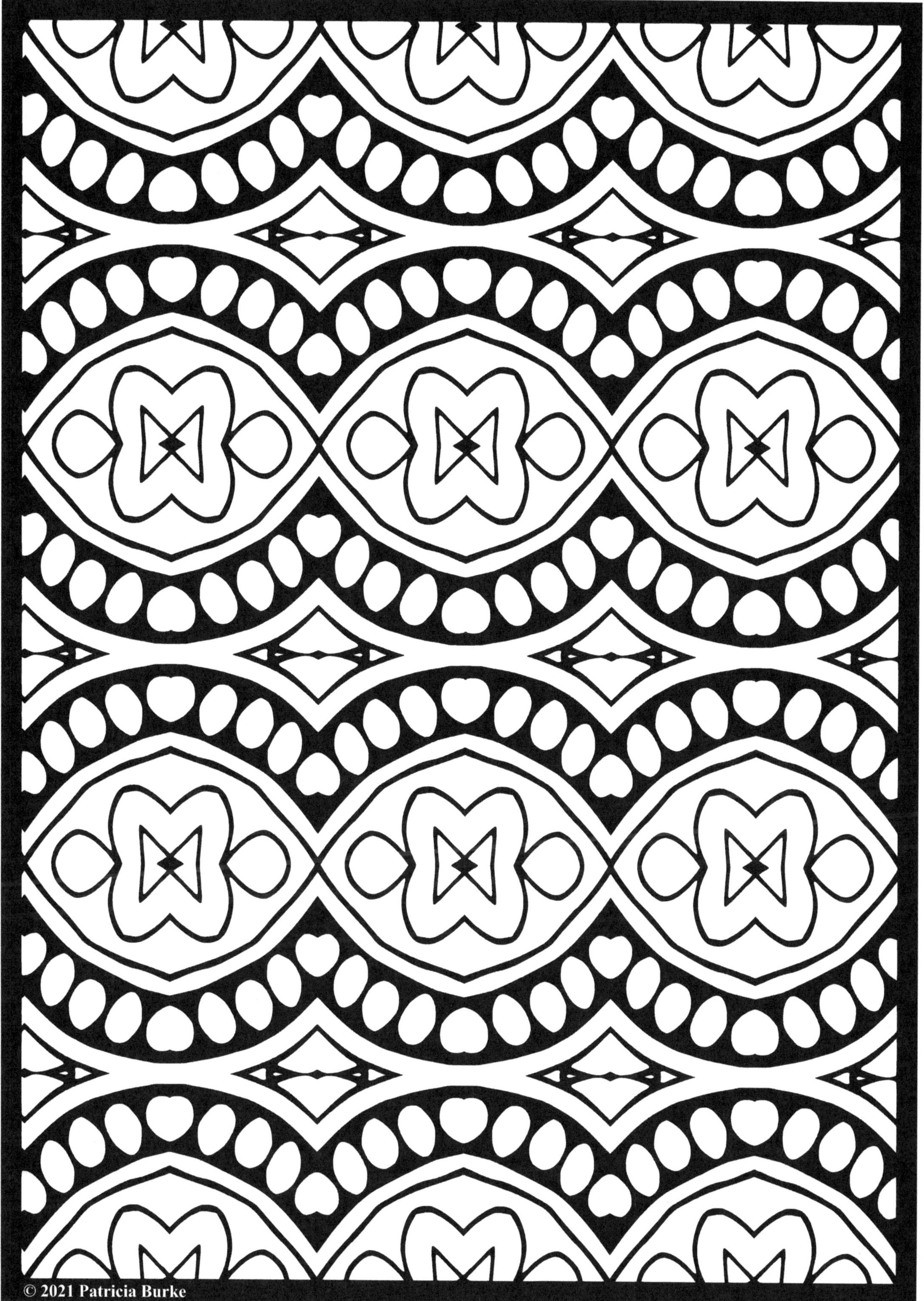

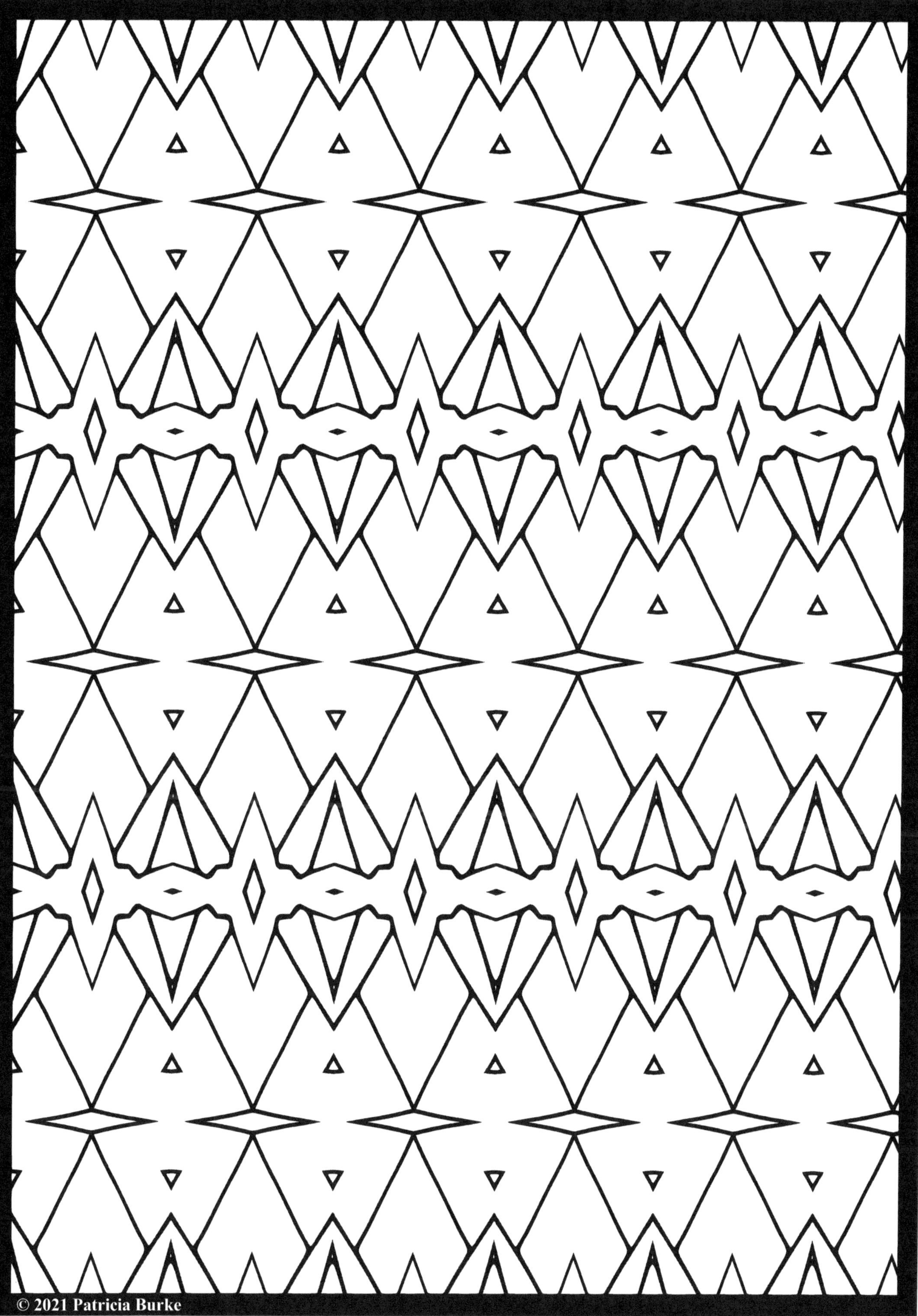

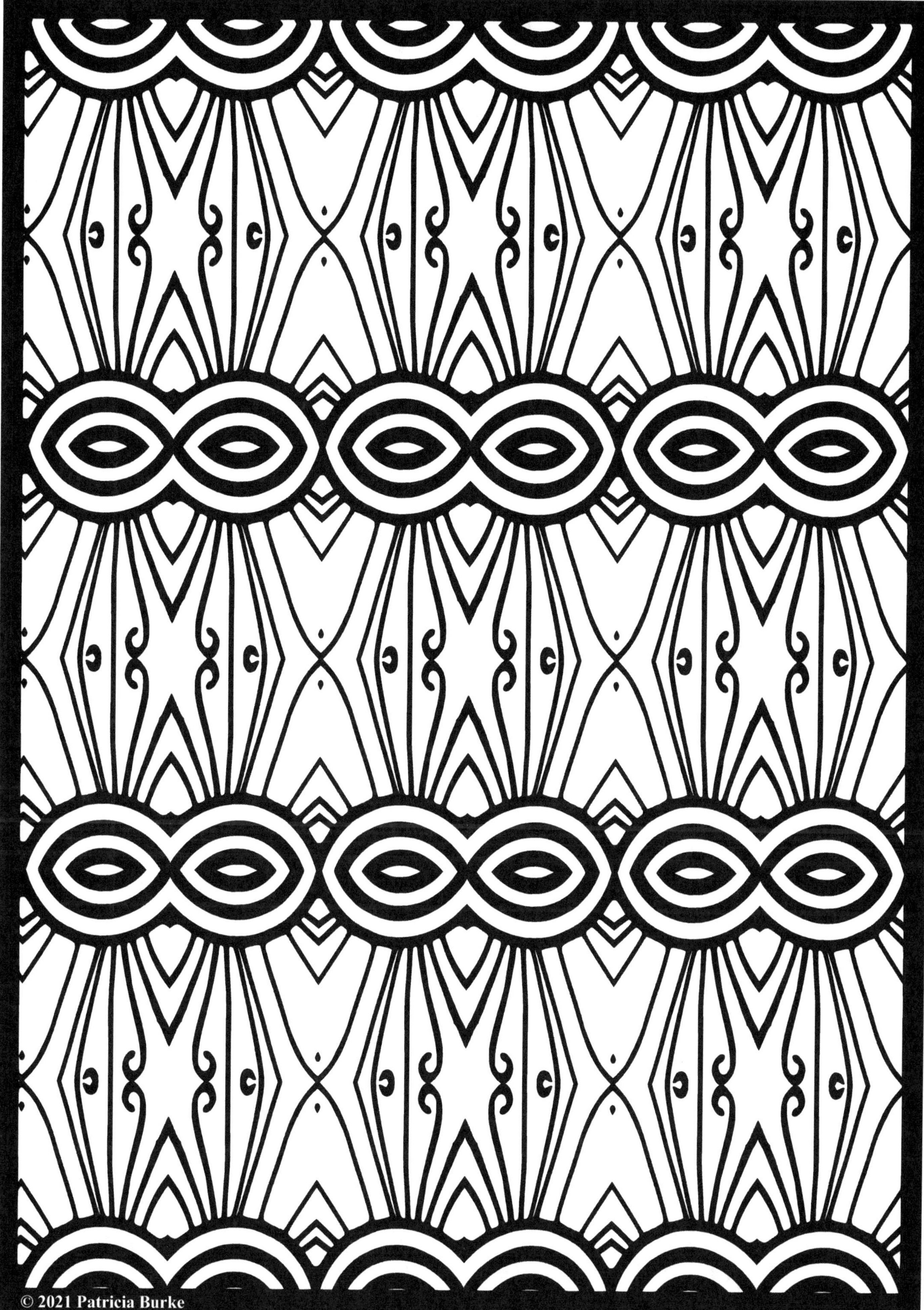

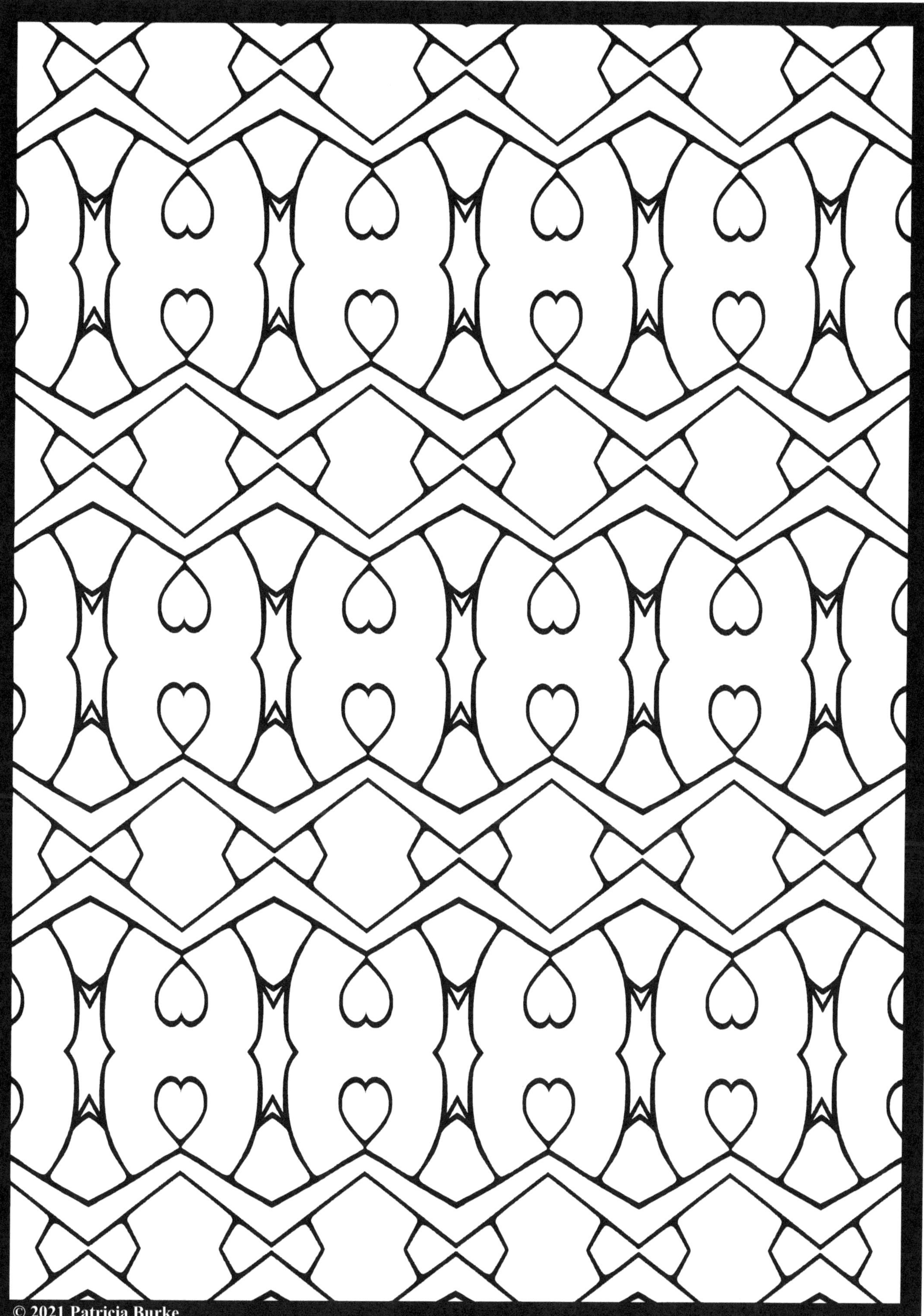

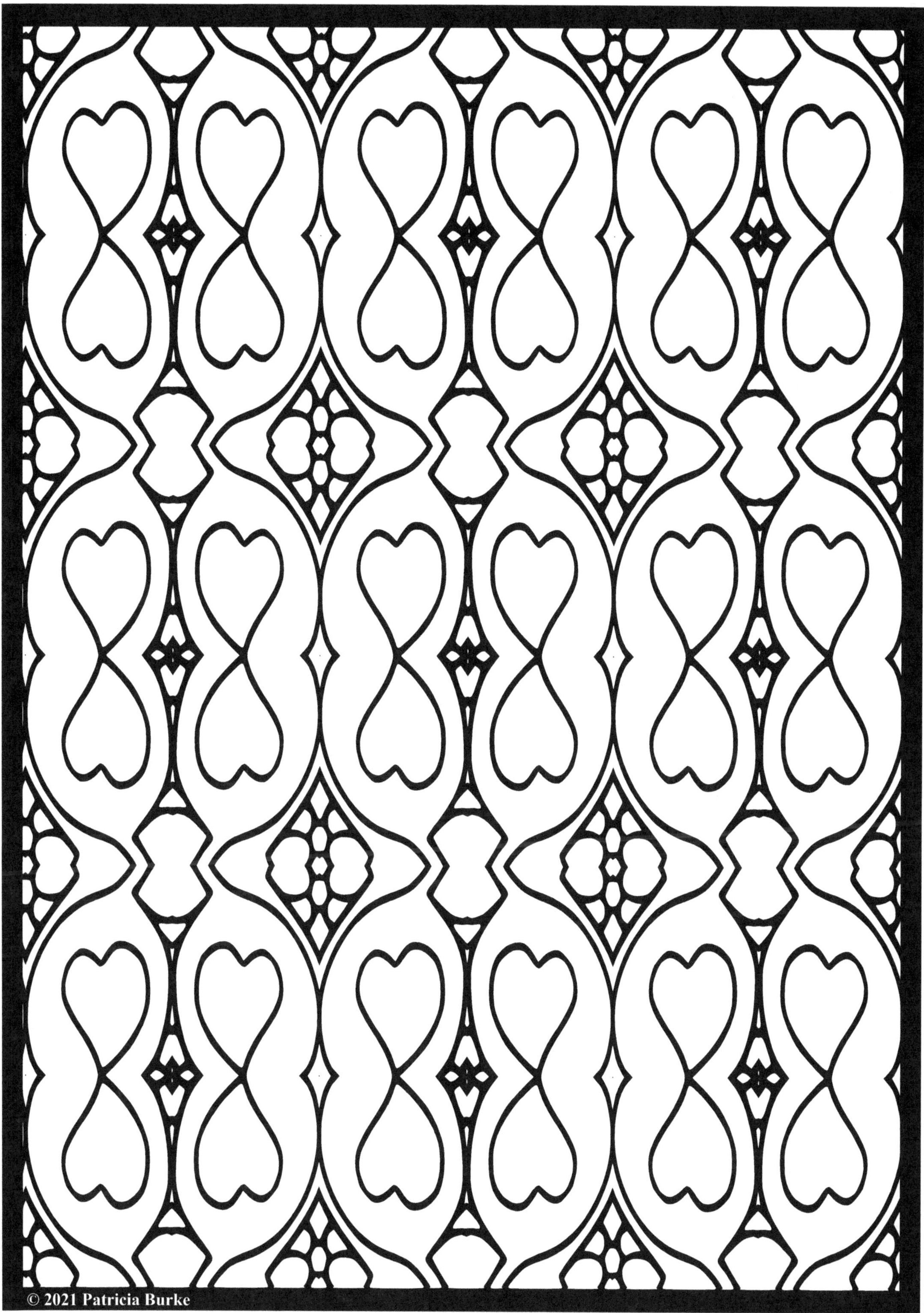

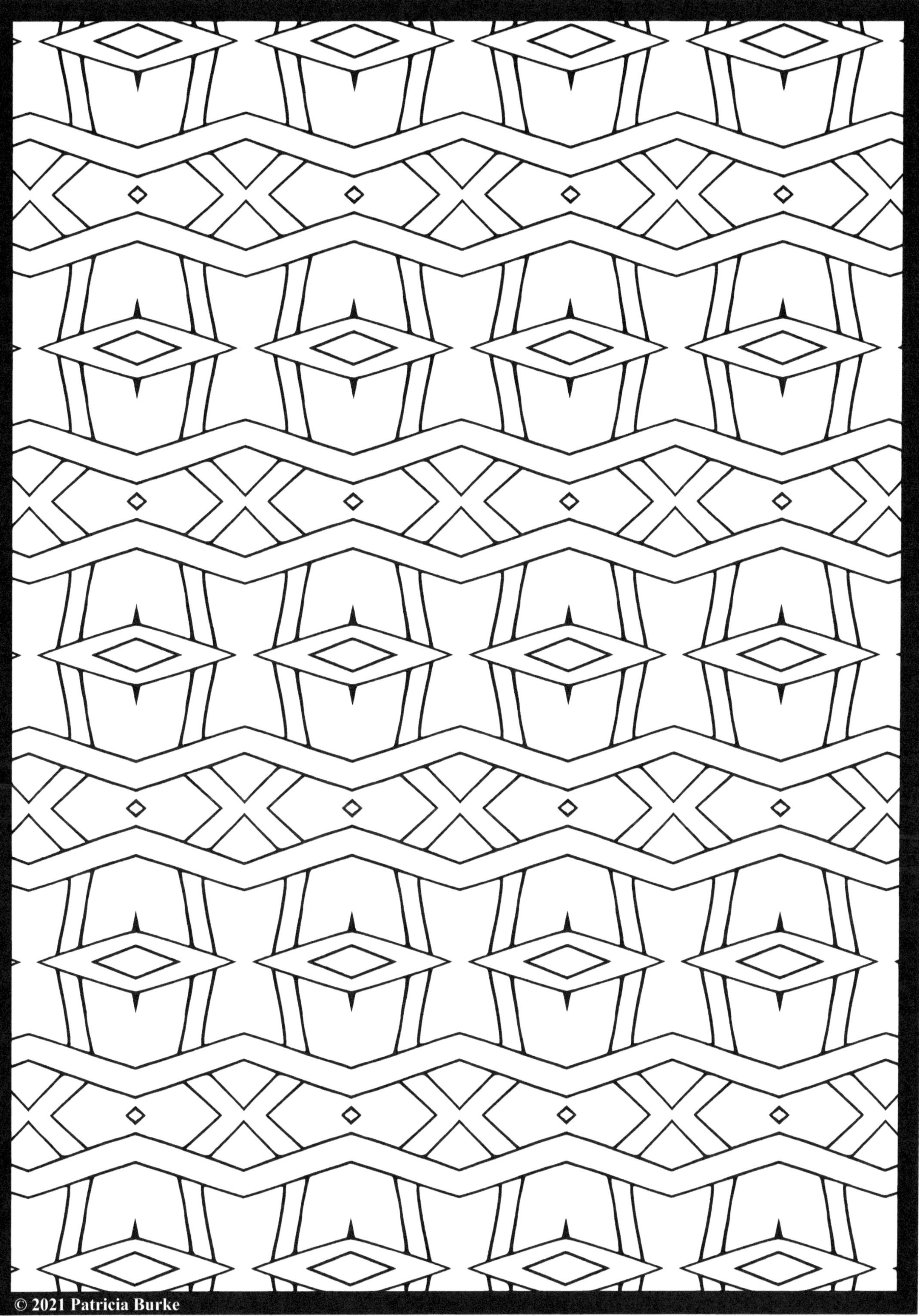

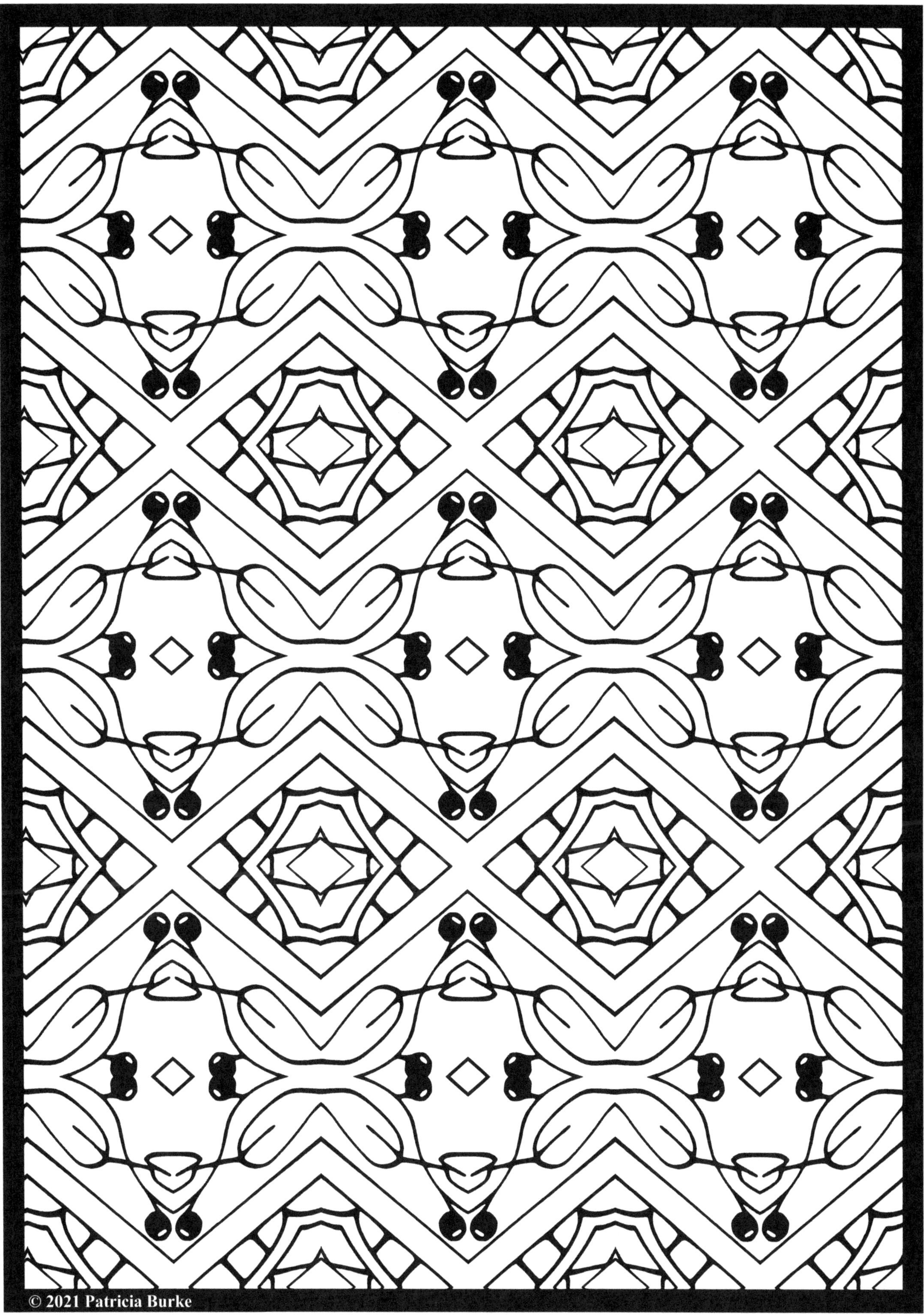

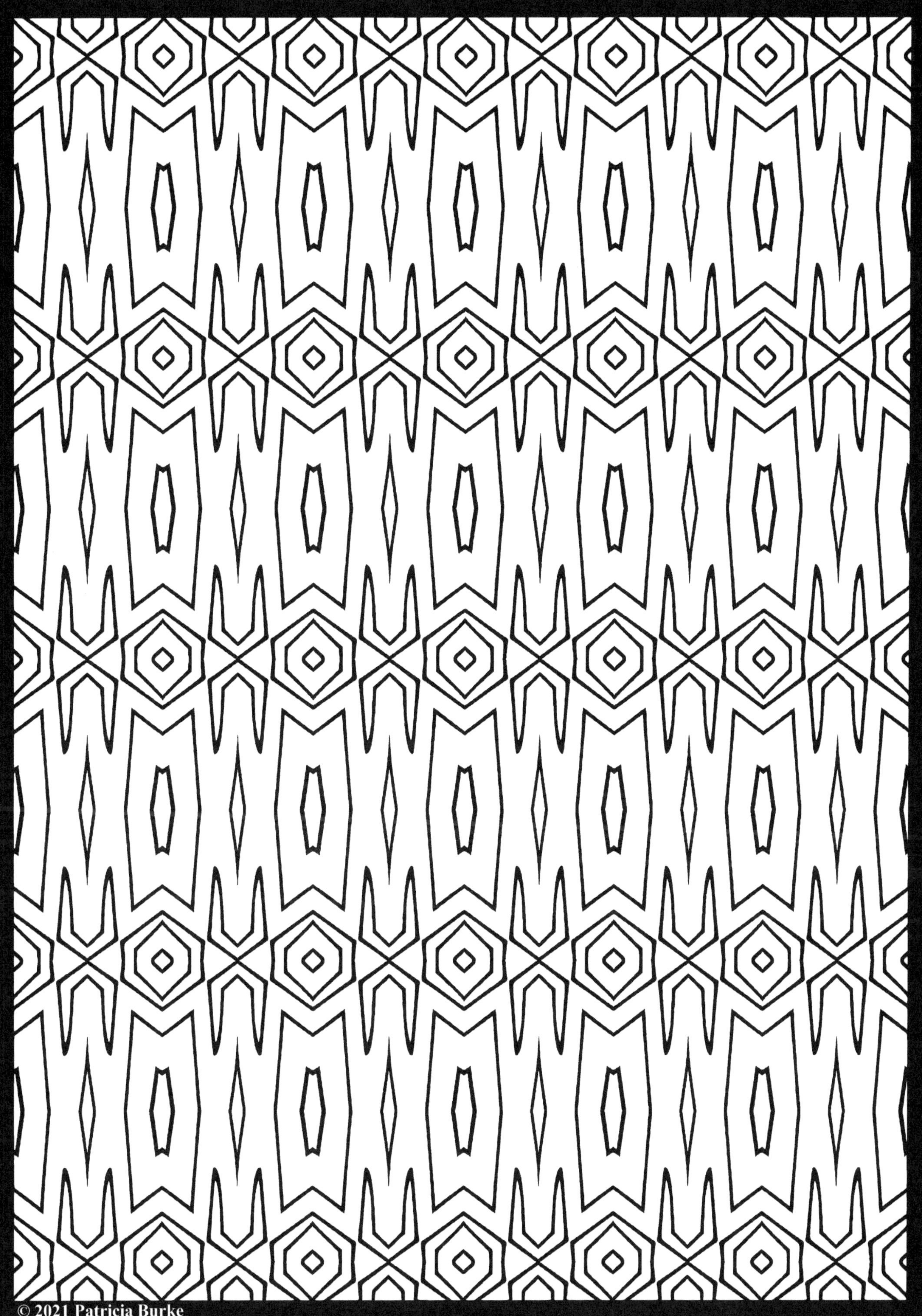

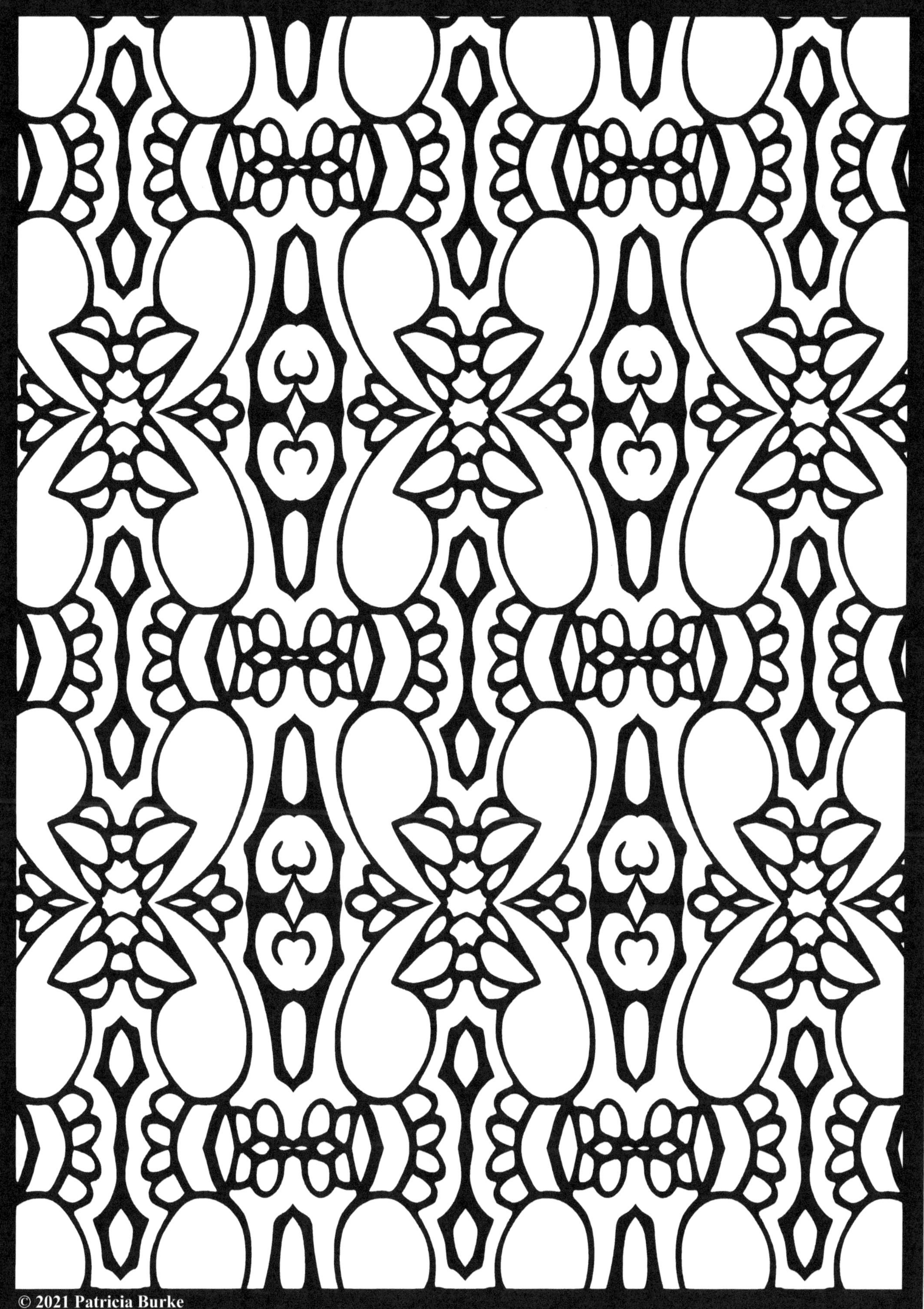

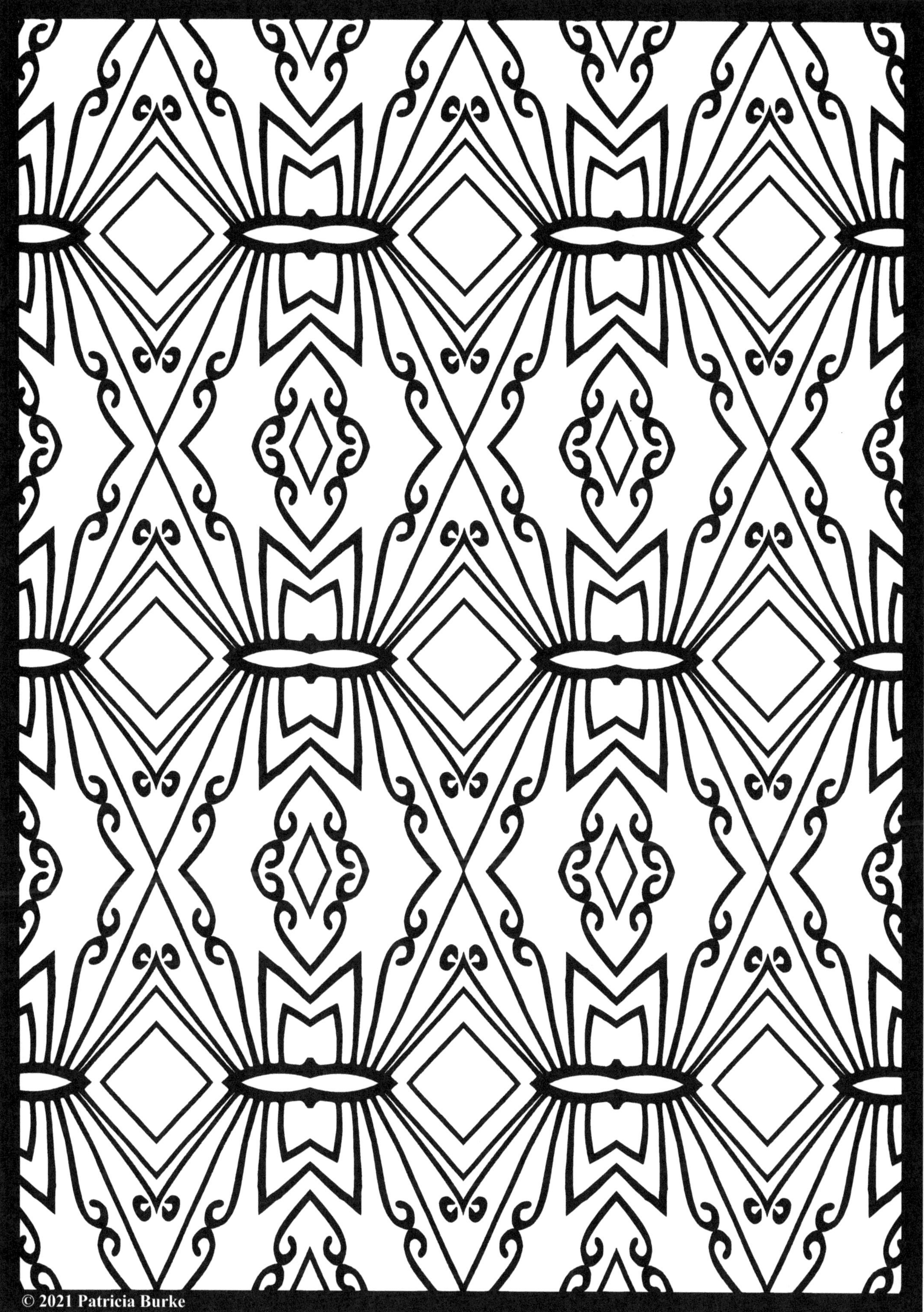

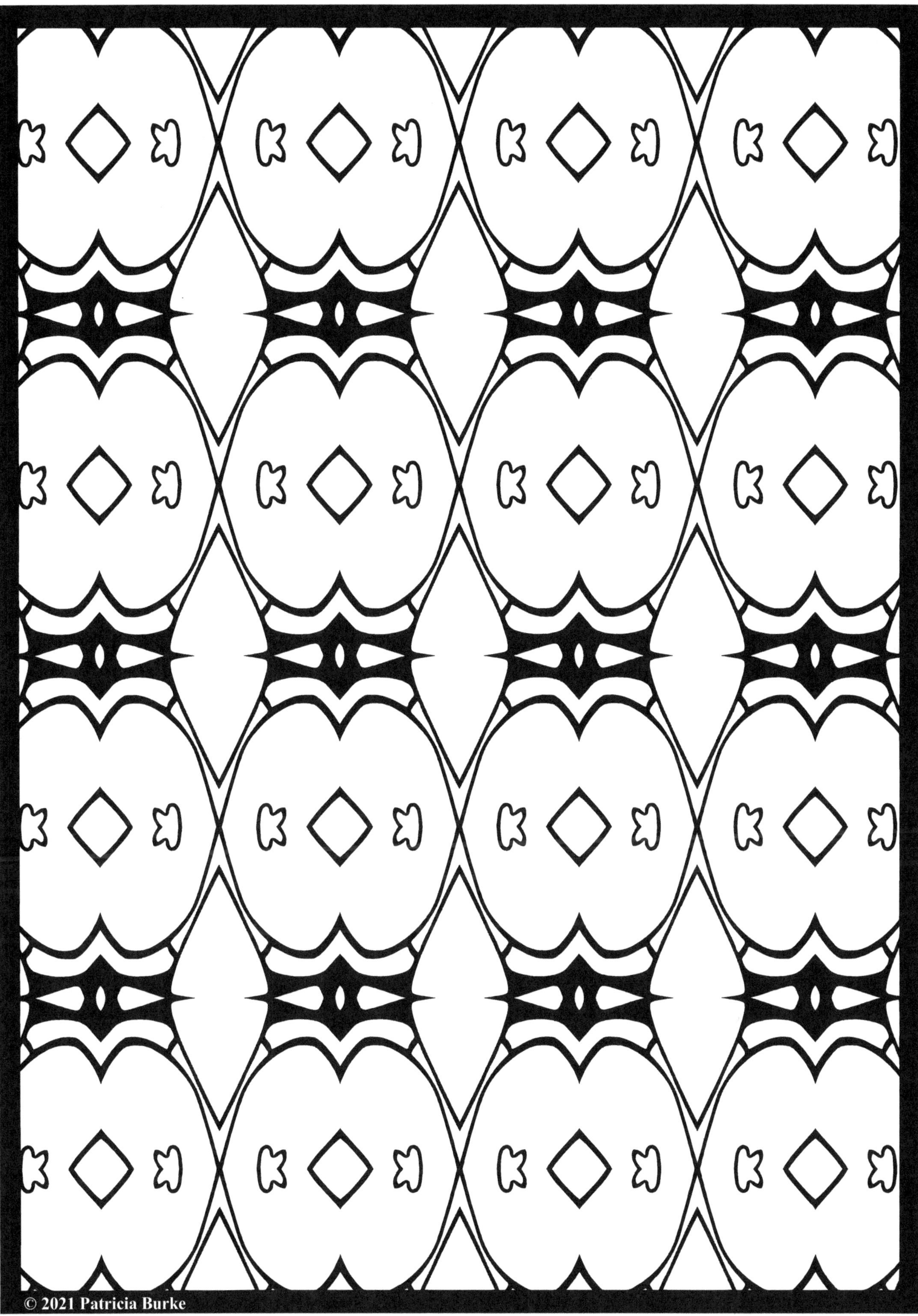

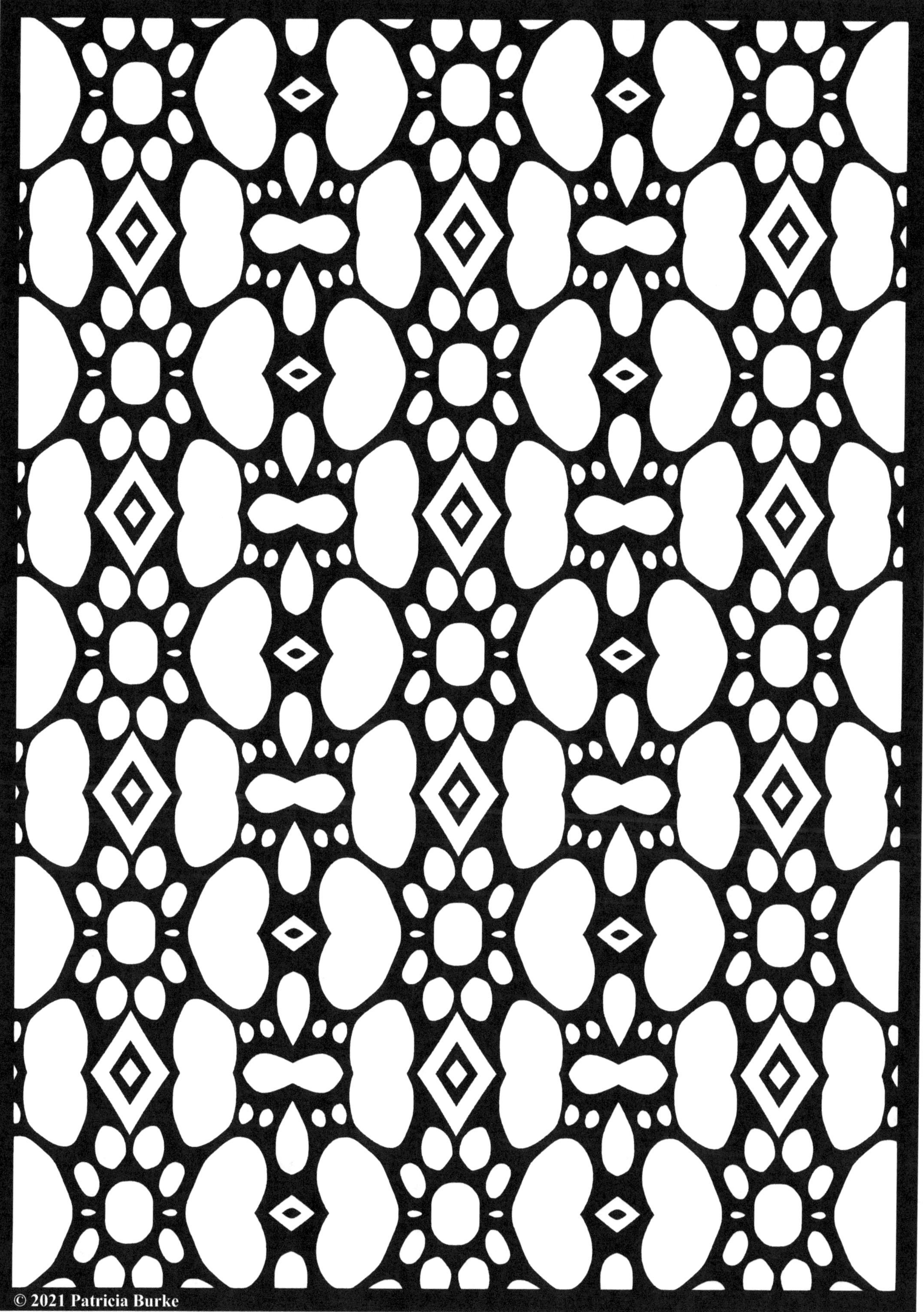

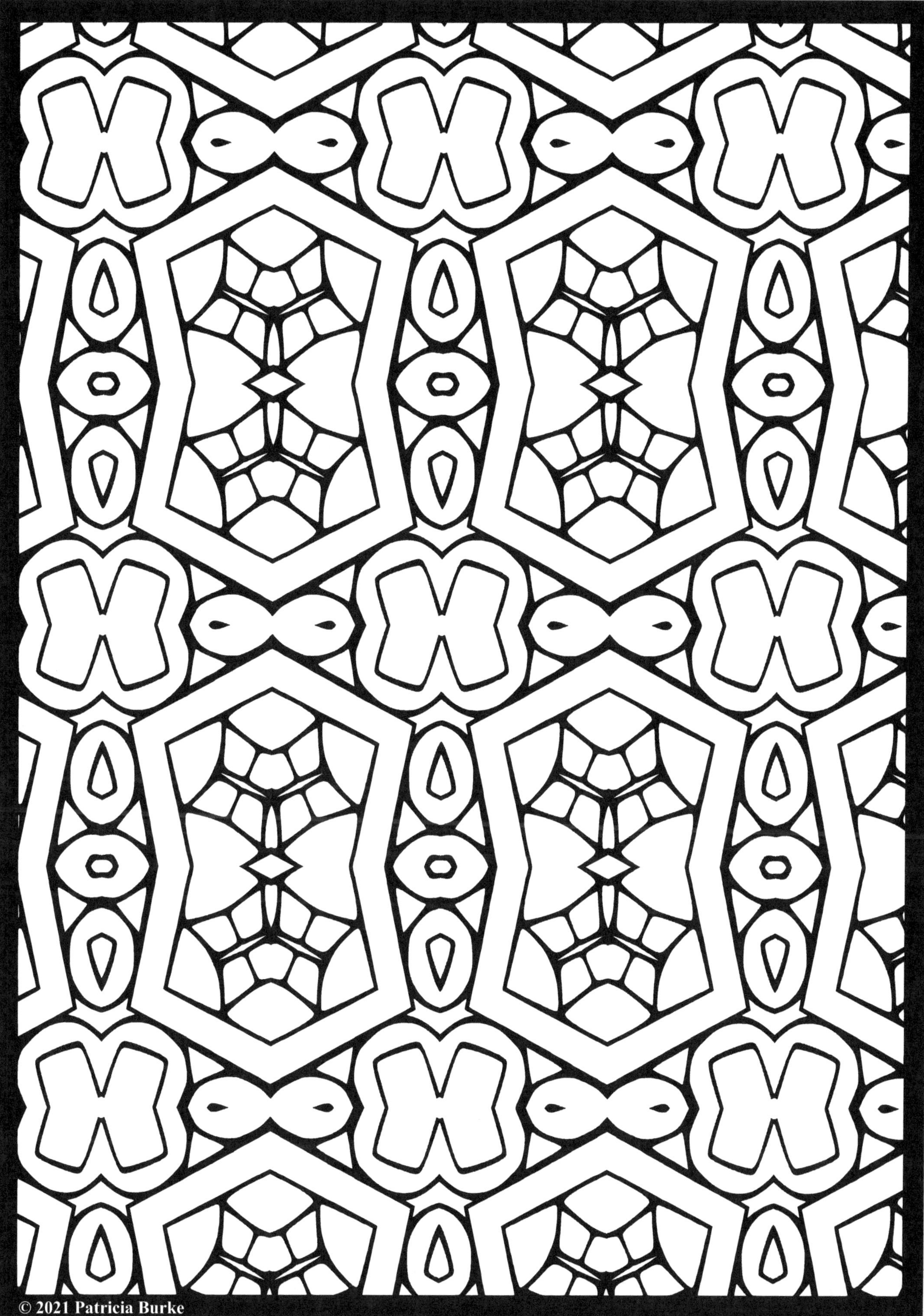

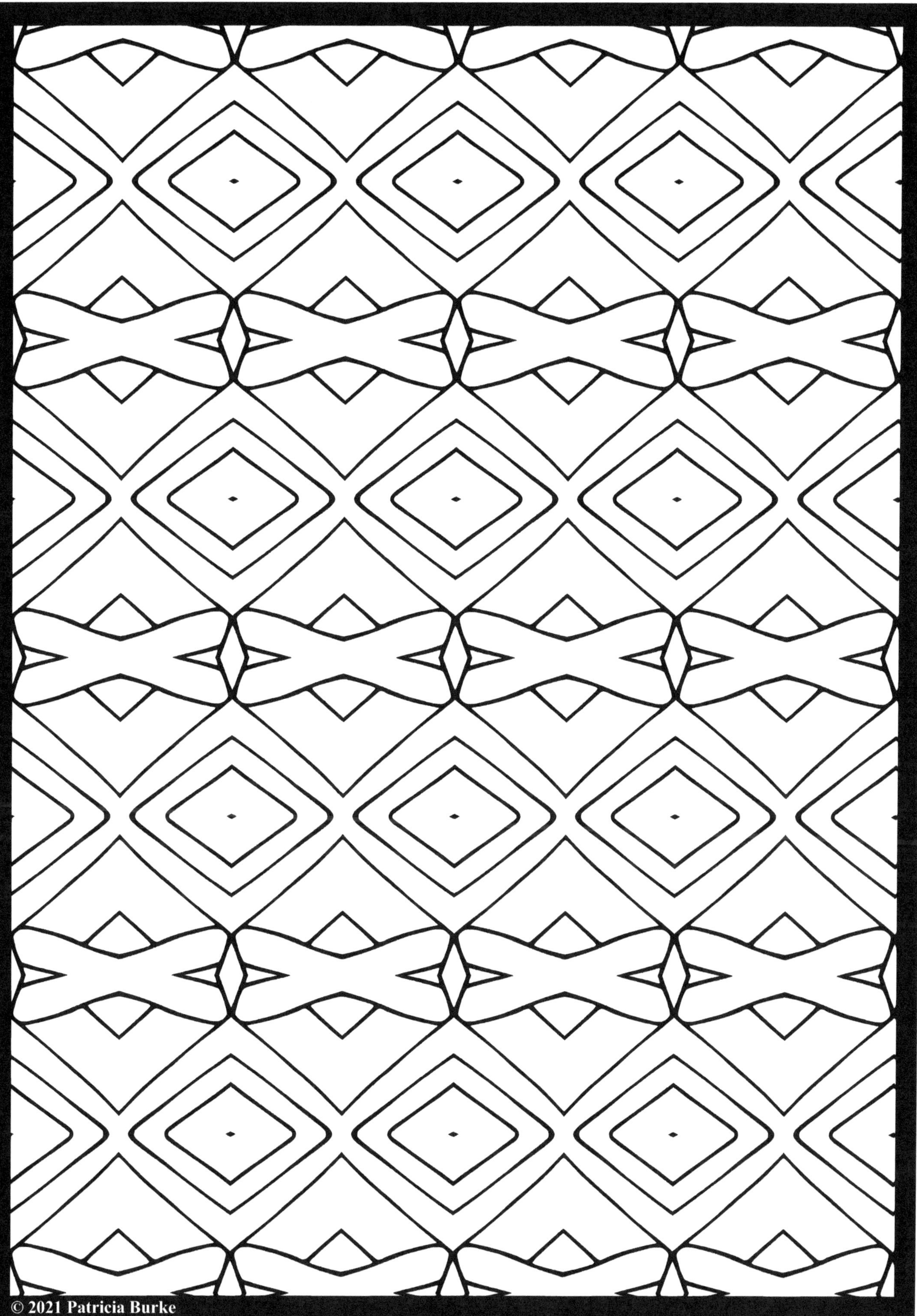

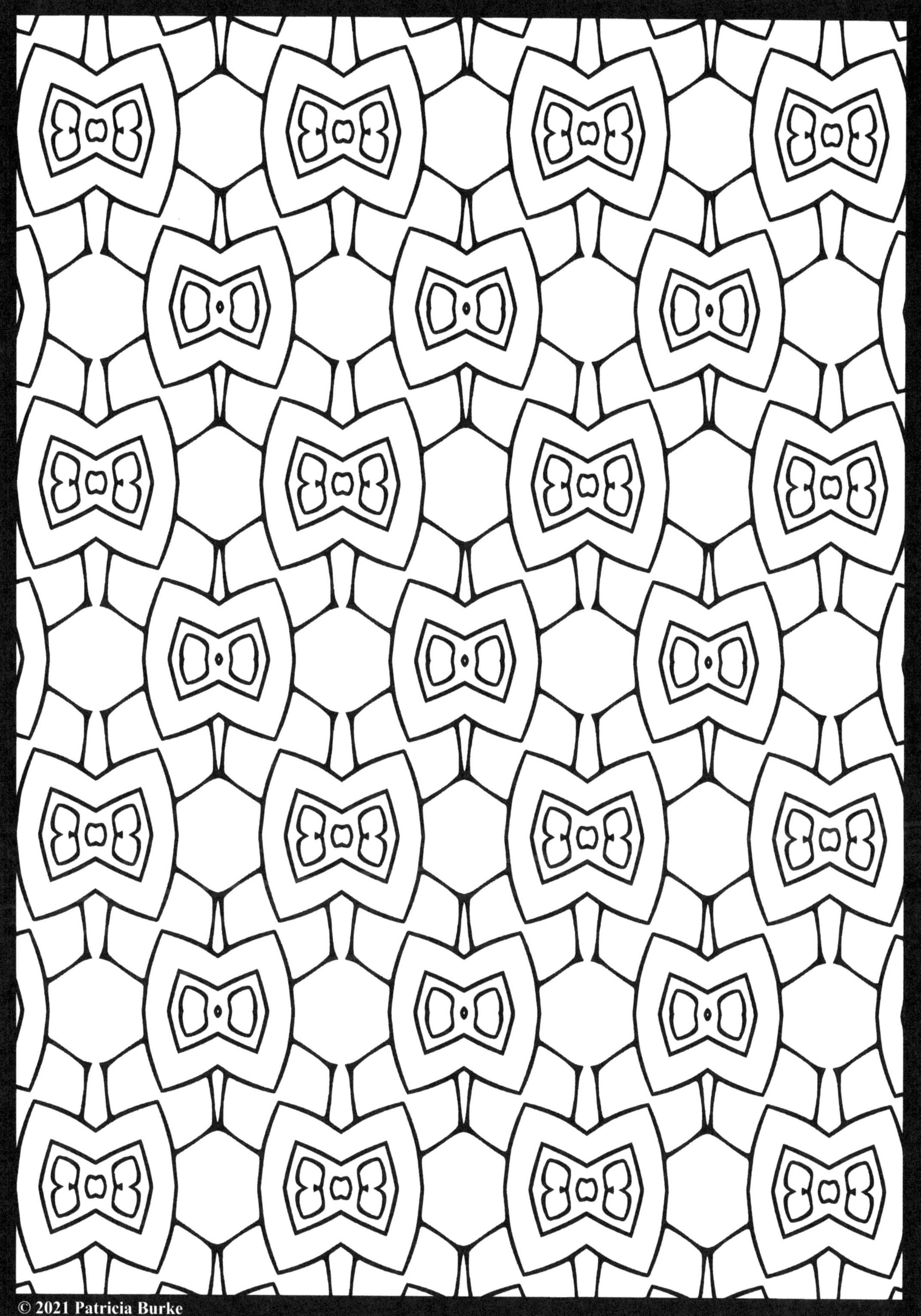

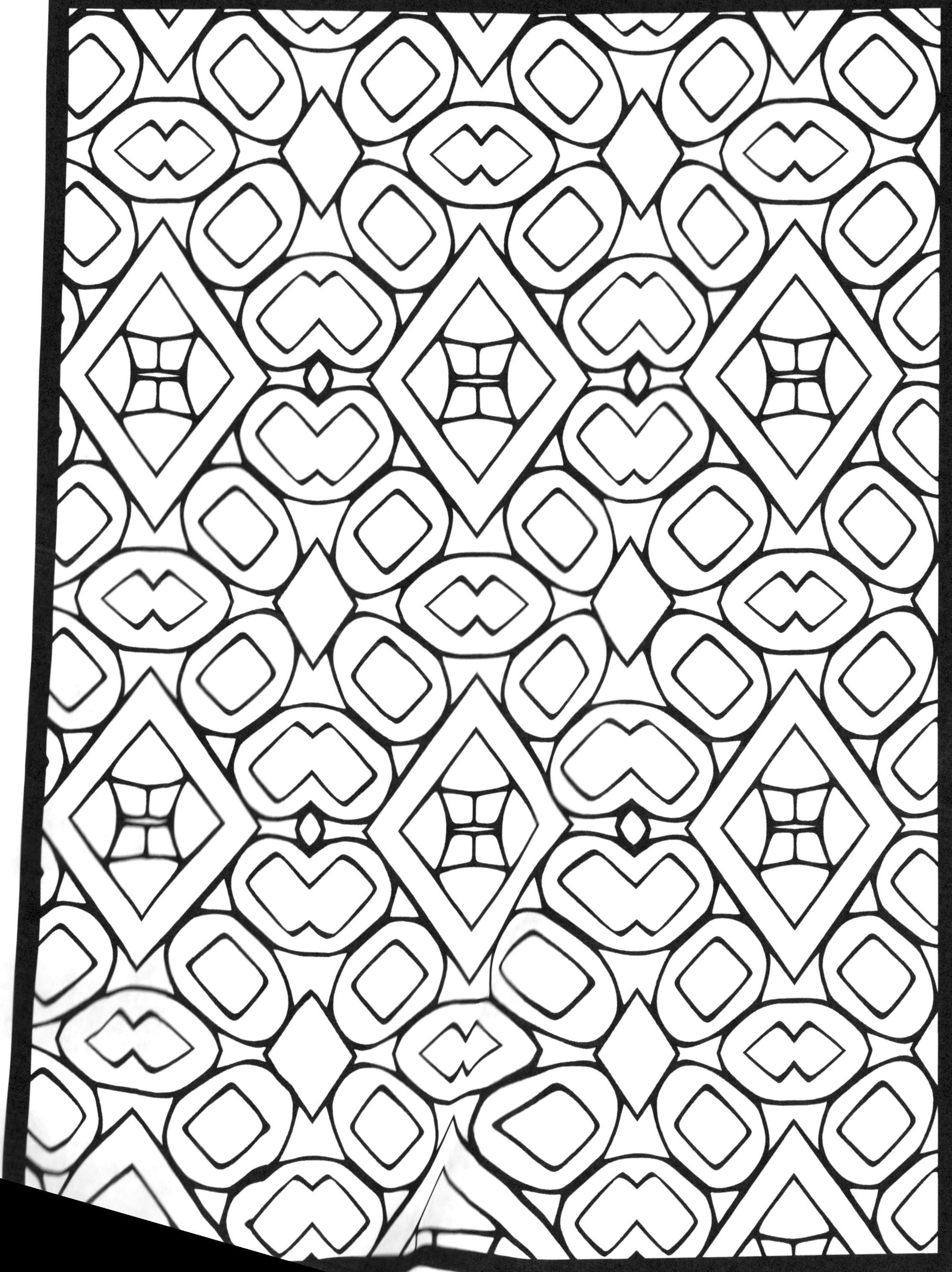

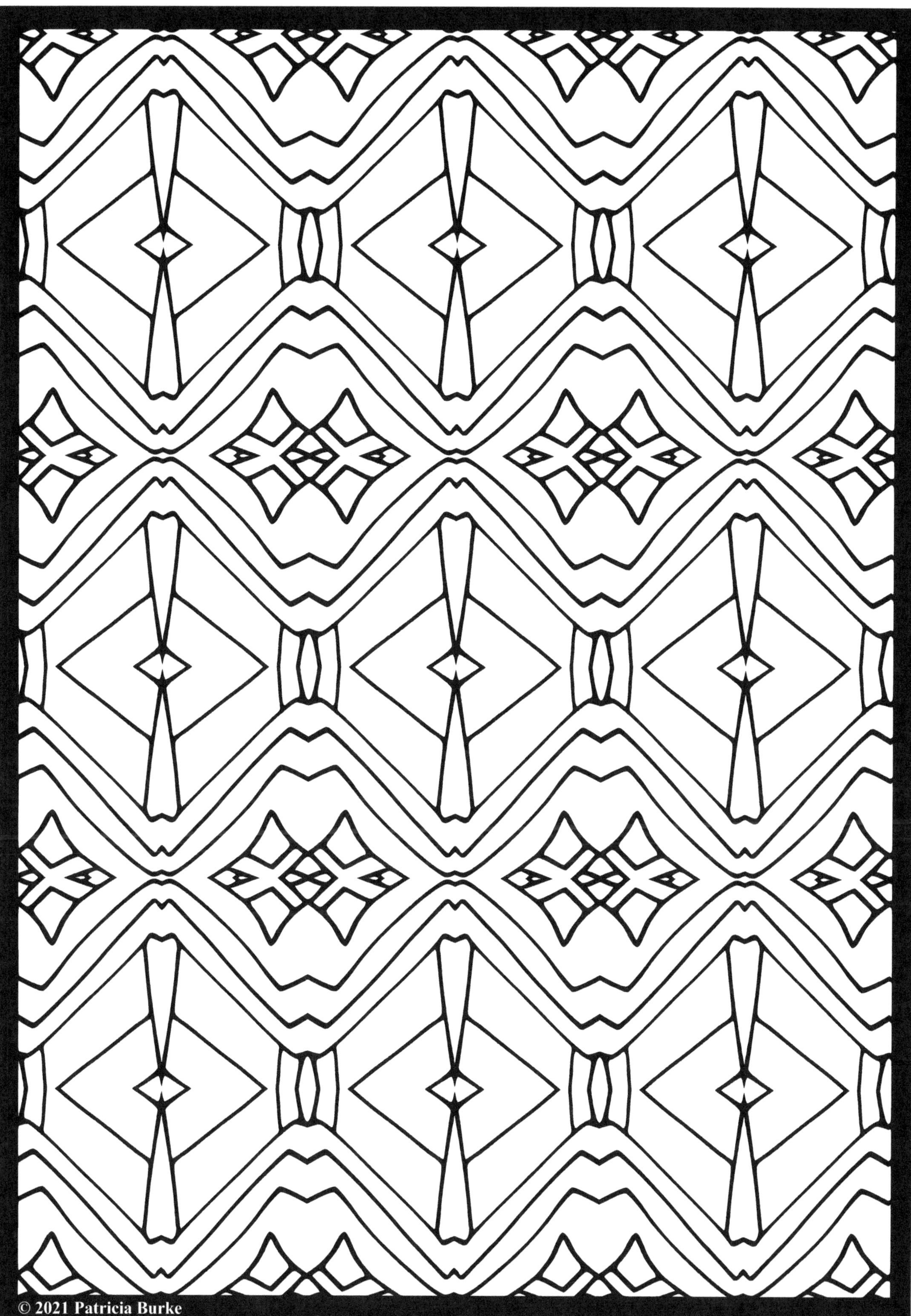

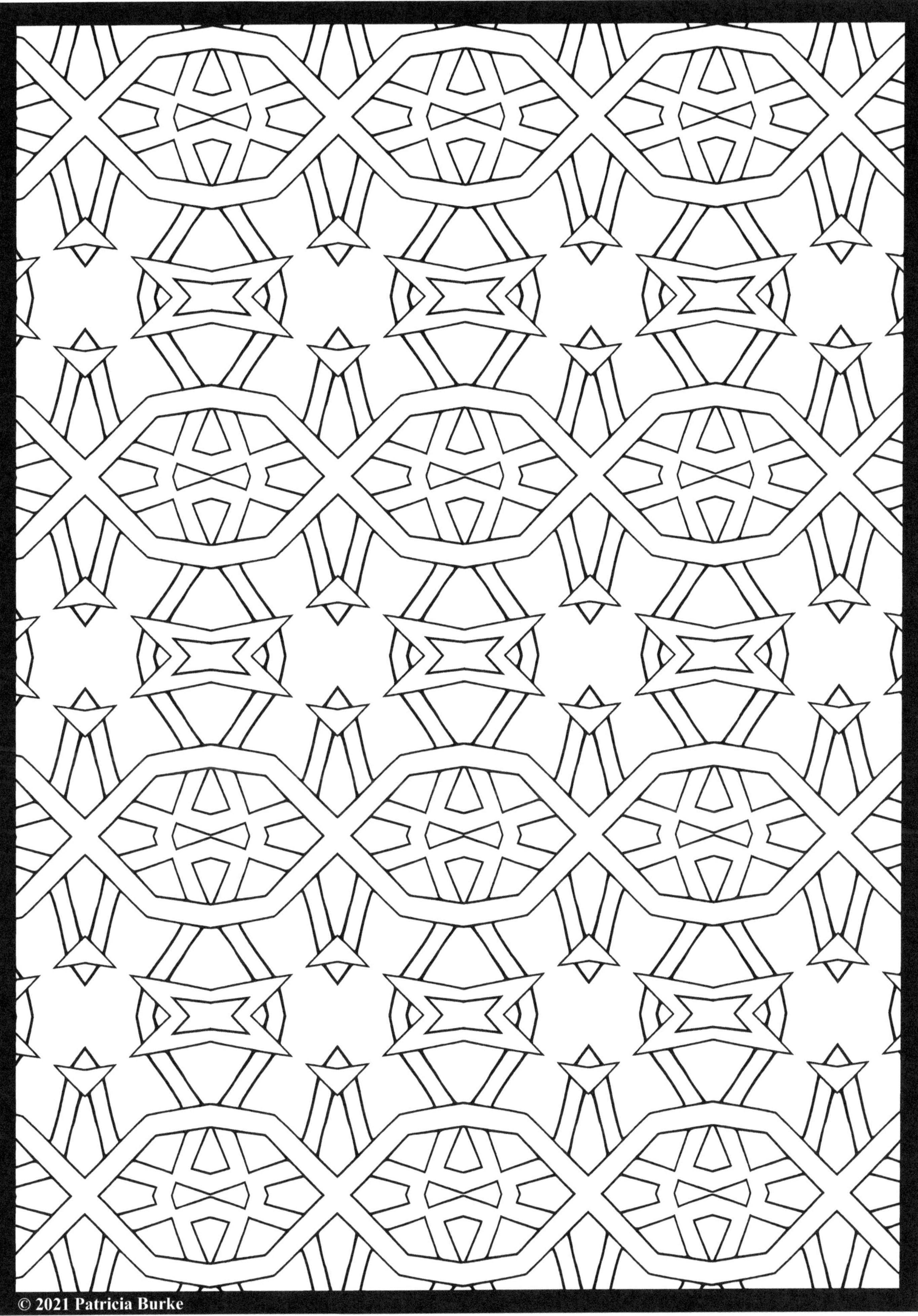

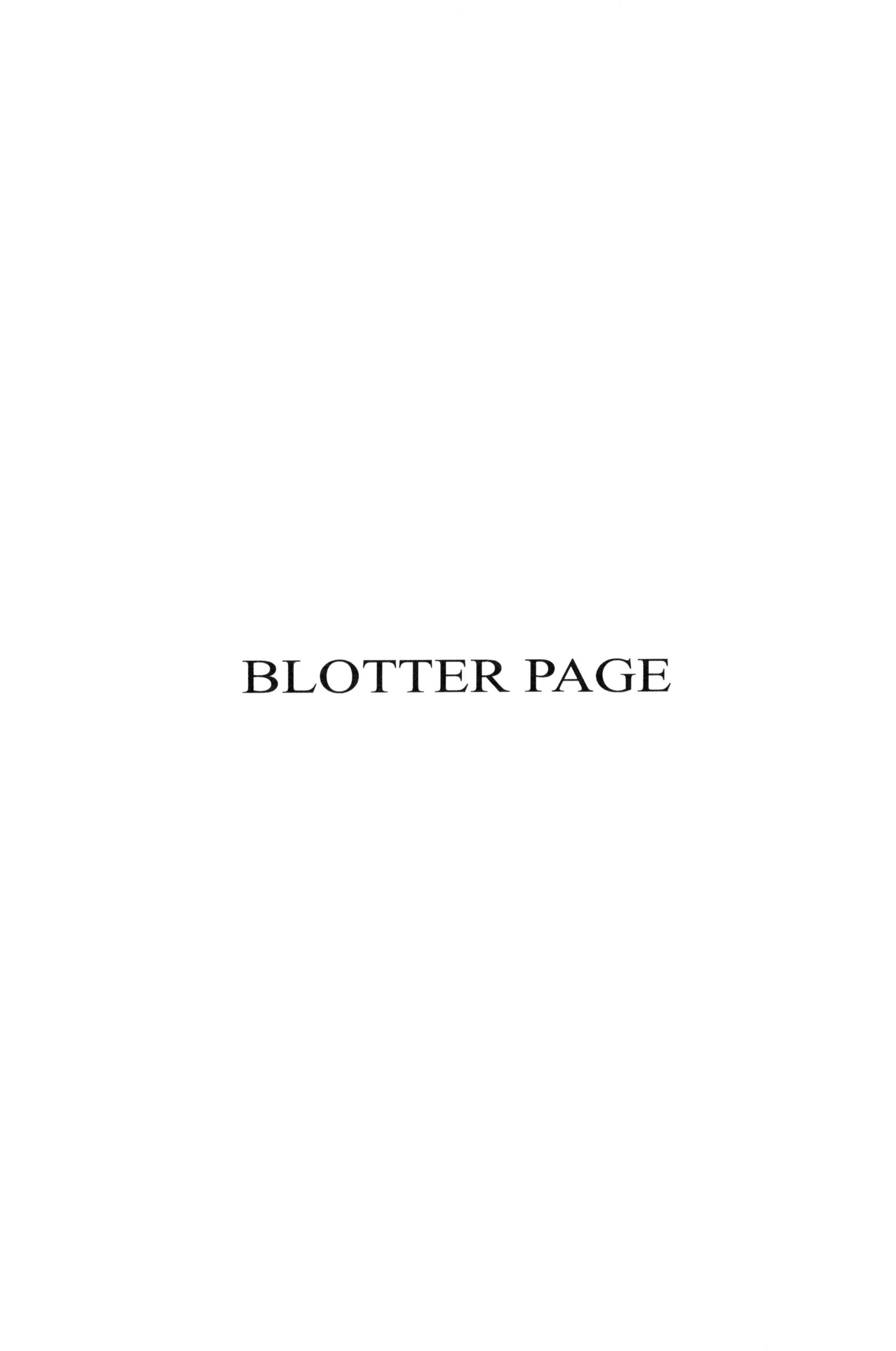

BLOTTER PAGE

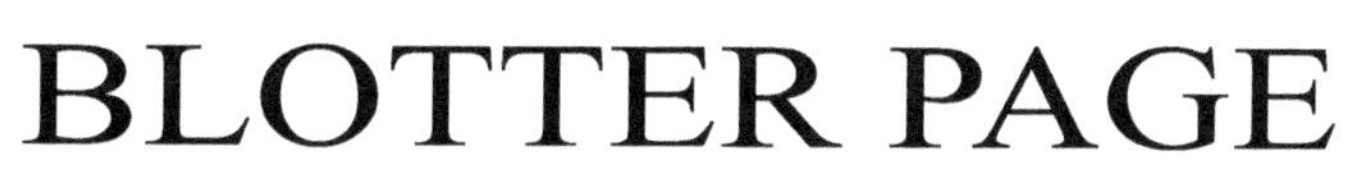
BLOTTER PAGE

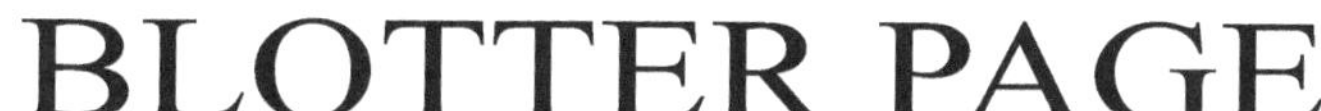

www.ingramcontent.com/pod-product-compliance
Lightning Source LLC
LaVergne TN
LVHW080923110826
845155LV00039B/198
* 9 7 8 1 9 5 1 5 7 6 1 2 7 *